It All Adds Up

The Growth of Victor Comptometer Corporation

Albert C. Buehler, Victor Comptometer chairman,
with new Series 10 electro-mechanical printing calculator.
Portrait is of Carl Buehler, Victor founder.

It All Adds Up

The Growth of Victor Comptometer Corporation

BY EDWIN DARBY

Library of Congress
Catalog Card Number
68-58916

Because of the remarkable growth of Victor Comptometer Corporation, its directors determined to record its progress in book form. For the benefit of future corporate officers and students of business, the directors also determined to record the business philosophy or business principles adopted largely by Mr. A. C. Buehler, chairman of the board, which directed such unusual growth. For that purpose, they engaged Mr. Edwin Darby, financial editor of the Chicago Sun-Times, independently to study, appraise, and record the facts. He has written his findings in this book.

VERNON R. LOUCKS
General Counsel
and Member,
Board of Directors

CONTENTS

It All Adds Up

The Growth of Victor Comptometer Corporation

CHAPTER 1

A. C. Buehler Reminisces

I wasn't very healthy as a kid. I suffered from asthma and bronchitis and contracted pneumonia when I was three. That's the reason we spent our winters from 1900 to 1912 in San Antonio, Texas. We went south in October and returned in June.

I'm the oldest, stand five feet three, and I'm still called Shorty, even by my eleven grandchildren. H.L., known as Slim, is almost six feet. R.O., or Bob, is about five feet nine. Butts, who is now deceased, was baptized Christian, an old family name, and he stood five eight. Being the first and shortest, I always accused

Mother of practicing on me and then doing a better job on the other boys. We had no sisters, but had an older brother who lived only a few days.

At first Mother—her name was Rose—Slim and I made the trip south. The other boys joined us as they came along. At the beginning, we rented a couple of rooms in the home of a local family. As we increased our numbers we rented a small house. During our last few years in San Antone, as the natives call it, we owned a small home with a large yard. The folks thought four boys needed plenty of room. We didn't see Dad—his name was Carl—during our Texas stays, until about 1910. Frankly, he couldn't afford the time or money to make the trip. He and his two brothers were each operating a meat market, as a partnership, known as Buehler Bros. It was quite a financial struggle to get started and with a family in Texas, he didn't have much left to live on.

To keep expenses at a minimum and within his meager budget, he lived in an attic room. The only heat he had was what escaped from the floor below. He spent his evenings at the store, in the cashier's booth—the only place that had any heat. I recall him saying that nights on his walk from the store to his room, without an overcoat, he was often tempted to help himself to one when he passed a man who looked as if he could afford another.

It was very scenic down in San Antone with the trees and parks and the river and the old missions. In those days Arizona wasn't very much or we'd probably have gone there. We go to the San Marcos in Chandler, Arizona now. It's the oldest resort in Arizona and it is only 50 years old. San Antone was already a place where Texans retired. When they wanted to get out of a ranch town, they'd go to San Antonio.

I remember the river that ran through town. We used to swim in that river. We had a place on the bend where the river was wider and deeper with the water rushing around the curve there was a

Carl and Rose Buehler in 1930
with their four sons, from left:
Christian C., Herman L.,
Robert O., and Albert C.

cave right above it. I remember in late May or early June we'd swim down there and we'd leave a dime up above on the top of a post beside the road. There was an old guy who'd drive down the road with a wagonload of watermelons to sell. He'd see the dime and he'd start a watermelon down the hill and it would hit the water and we'd dive in—tear it apart—eat it and just throw the rind in the river and let it float away. A dime back there in 1907 or '08 was something. If a fellow was making $25 a week, he was getting good money.

My father's parents came from Germany. I don't know about my mother's family; she was an orphan. But my dad's folks came from Stuttgart and I've been able to trace the family back to 1604, about 13 generations. First the name was spelled Bihler and then the Germans changed their spelling a little and they got the "u" with the little dots over it. When the family came over to this country they dropped the dots and put in an "e" and the pronunciation was Americanized. My father used the American pronunciation, but my mother insisted on the old German sound. Sometimes they'd go to a social gathering and people would be interested and ask, "Are you two related?"

My grandfather—he was Christian Buehler—came over here and became a packer, a small meat packer, in Peoria. My dad started out as a paper salesman for an outfit in Peoria, but then he and two of his brothers conceived the idea of starting a chain of markets. So they came up to Chicago and opened one on Chicago Avenue and one on Madison Street on the West side and one on Lincoln Avenue on the Northwest.

Then they started stores out of town. The younger brother, who was named Herman, went to Cleveland and started running stores in and around there. And the other brother, who was named Christian after my grandfather, decided to go back to his home town, Peoria, and he opened some stores in the Peoria area. My father stayed with the Chicago stores but expanded further into Illinois, Indiana, Wisconsin and Michigan. I know he had stores in Grand Rapids and Kalamazoo and Niles and Bay City in Michigan and about 40 other locations. Then later he opened up about 15 stores in Canada.

I guess you'd say this was unusual; they must have had one of the very first chain store operations. And they had then what we'd now call central purchasing. I remember going over to the railroad siding at the old Chicago Stockyards and there would be seven or eight refrigerator railroad cars lined up there. The different packers would bring their stuff up and my dad or someone would tell them where to put it—"this goes in this car for Anderson and Muncie and that goes in that car for Richmond and Indianapolis." They had a system worked out. Several cars would go out twice a week and there'd be instructions for drop shipments along the line at the cities where they had stores.

This chain operation was particularly unusual because they had a perishable item and didn't have the modern refrigerated cars. They'd just throw a few hundred pounds of ice in and let her go.

In the early years when there were just the three stores and the three brothers, they had an unusual way of keeping the company books, too. Each brother would keep his own books. At the end of the year, each would sit down and figure out how much profit his own store had made. Then he'd send each of the other two brothers a check for one-third of his store's profit. They didn't have any combined bookkeeping and they didn't audit each other. This worked for a time, but Herman wasn't too ambitious about expanding his operations out in Cleveland, and Chris had a chance to buy an old packing firm in Peoria called E. Godle & Sons. Chris wanted it and it meant a lot to him—you know, he was a Peoria boy, and here was a chance to take over the oldest packing house in town.

Then, too, there was the fact that Dad had four children and the other two didn't have children, so that it was getting a little uneven as far as the earnings were concerned. They finally decided that each would keep his own stores, his own operations and his own profits.

After some years Herman passed away and his widow more or less disposed of the stores to people who worked for him. Then Christian died and his estate went to his wife. His wife left the estate to build The Christian Buehler Memorial Home in Peoria. It is quite an institution. His string of markets is still running and the profits go to the old people's home.

My dad went right on building. Many of the stores are still operating today under the original name, Buehler Bros. My brother, H.L., runs them. Some are real supermarkets now, but some are still meat markets with a line of canned goods. I remember Dad even had a couple of stores up in Minnesota, and when I went up there I rode in one of the first buses that later was to become the Greyhound Line. It was a Buick sedan with what was then called a winter top—side curtains instead of windows—and it ran between a couple of old mining towns and Duluth.

I don't know whether or not you would have classified Dad as a millionaire. He did get so he was making well over $100,000 a year when there was little or no income tax. He had enough. And he gave generously. You know, my mother was born here in Chicago. She was about eight days old when the great Chicago fire took place. They took the mattress off the bed and put it in one of those big, highsided wagons and put her and her mother on the mattress. They threw a blanket over the top of the wagon and wetted it down and made a run for it out to the edge of town. Out there they turned the wagon over so that the floor served as a roof and they lived inside that highsided wagon until things got back to some semblance of order in town.

My mother was orphaned very early in her life and she was raised in the Uhlich Children's Home, now located at 3737 North Mozart Street, in the old German section on the Northwest side of Chicago. So Dad later got interested in the orphanage and the Lutheran parish there, St. Paul's. He gave them a block of ground and told them he'd give them $100,000 for a new building if the parish would raise another $100,000. Finally they raised the money and Dad sat down and wrote a check for the $100,000 with the indelible pencil he carried—he always had trouble with fountain pens. Later the church decided to build an old people's home and he gave a block of ground for that, too, and I don't know how much money. St. Paul's was where all the old German families went—the Oscar Mayers and the Wieboldts and so on—and up to eight or ten years ago they'd still have one Sunday church service in German. They still do have services in German in the chapel, which is called the Buehler Chapel. Dad died in 1932, so it was in the 1920s that he was helping the church raise the money.

My mother was a strong one, a little dynamo. She had her own opinions and she made us toe the mark. She was an energetic woman, she worked hard, and she expected everyone else to work hard. I guess it didn't hurt me a bit. We had to learn how to cook ordinary meals—you know, fry a pork chop or make bacon and eggs—and we had to make our beds, and we had to learn how to press a suit. "Maybe," she said, "we won't always have the money to get a suit pressed for us." She lived past 75 and she was still going strong. I remember when she was in her 70s, she'd be sick, have a cold or something, but come the monthly Frauen Verein meeting at the church, she'd be there. She'd be there or else.

Dad was a worker, too, of course. He was also a planner and he had a pretty good imagination; he had to have in order to see the possibilities in the adding machine business, which was a far cry from the meat business.

CHAPTER 2

Meat Markets + Adding Machines

Victor Comptometer Corporation. Executive office: 3900 North Rockwell Street, Chicago, Illinois 60618. Eighteen plants in the United States and Canada. Direct sales outlets in nearly 80 nations in the free world. Net sales volume: approximately $150,000,000. Shareholders: over 5,000 of record. Number of employees: more than 8,000. Chairman: Albert C. Buehler. Vice Chairman: Raymond J. Koch. President: Alvin F. Bakewell. Executive Vice President: Albert C. Buehler, Jr. Treasurer: Vincent G. McDonagh. Secretary: Raymond F. Koch. Founder: Carl Buehler, father of A.C. and grandfather of A.C., Jr. This was Victor Comptometer

Corporation in its 50th anniversary year of 1968.

Carl Buehler could figure about anything in his head. He could total a column of four digit items about as fast as he could read the numbers. And he could run a multimillion-dollar retail chain of nearly 100 meat markets, a pioneering operation in its day, out of his pockets. He did have an office, the headquarters of Buehler Bros. But it was not often that he sat behind his office desk. Aside from occasional visits to one or another of the meat markets, he had to keep an eye on the company's small meat processing and packing plant. But more demanding was the constant need to see to it that the markets in the chain were supplied with fresh meats. Carl Buehler would be at the stockyards buying beef and pork and lamb by 6:30 in the morning, so that the meat could be put aboard iced cars and shipped out for arrival early the following morning at the various Buehler Bros. shops in Illinois, Indiana, Minnesota, Michigan and Wisconsin.

Between the office, the stockyards, the railroad, and the stores, Carl was always on the move. In one pocket he carried a sheaf of bills and correspondence. In another he had a small account book and a check book. Maybe the day's mail had brought a check covering last week's receipts from the Elkhart, Indiana store for $2,565. Buehler would enter the payment in his account book and, totaling the current expenses of the Elkhart store, note the profit position. Or with a minute to spare and finding a bill from Swift & Co. in his pocket, he'd write out a check, put it in an envelope, also secured from a pocket, and drop it in the next mailbox he came to.

To a graduate of a college of business administration this may be an unthinkable method of operation. But obviously it worked for Carl Buehler—in a simpler age when, among other things, the federal income tax did not make the keeping of meticulous books a business necessity, and when the cost for new store fixtures was

Typical of Buehler meat markets was this Springfield, Ohio store (right). Poker-playing porkers in Anderson, Indiana window made up one of many displays that featured meat animals, an example of the family flair for merchandising.

an expense, not an item for depreciation. Nevertheless, Buehler, a man of rare foresight and imagination, was aware of the shortcomings of his pocket "system" and of Buehler Bros. accounting, starting as it did with a butcher wiping his hands on his white apron, taking his pencil from behind his ear and figuring up two pounds, three ounces at 36 cents a pound on a paper sack.

In any event, Carl Buehler was receptive when the salesman called on him one day in 1918 and began to talk about the practicality of an adding machine, how it was easy to operate and never made mistakes. Buehler listened, decided he would try one and handed the man a check in part payment. A few days later Buehler was shocked and understandably chagrined to receive not an adding machine, but, by mail, a certificate for 10 shares of stock in a company being formed to produce and sell a new, improved and less expensive adding machine. The amount of money was not great, only $100, but Carl Buehler was not accustomed to being flim-flammed. And he did want an adding machine.

The record is not clear, but apparently Buehler decided that his best bet for getting something, anything, for his money was to join the fledgling company, to take an interest in its affairs, and to try to get it off the ground. The State of Illinois had granted a charter to the Victor Adding Machine Co., "done at the City of Springfield this 8th day of March, A.D. 1918, and of the Independence of the United States the one hundred and 42nd." Capitalization: $100,000 with 10,000 shares of stock to be issued.

By summer of 1918 Carl Buehler had made his decision—and his commitment—to Victor. On September 3, 1918, he was elected a director. When Buehler attended his first stockholders' meeting (the company's second) on December 9, 1918, he already knew that things were not the best with the Victor Adding Machine Co. Cash was short, there were difficulties on the production line, sales were slow.

At that 1918 meeting, Buehler looked over his fellow stockholders and directors. More importantly, they looked him over. There was Oliver D. Johantgen, an Indiana farm boy and inventor who had spent most of his adult life up to that point attempting to design and perfect a radically different and improved adding machine. In return for 2,500 shares of Victor stock, he had assigned his patents to the company. An early financial backer of Johantgen's, George S. Eldred, also had received 2,500 shares for the interest he had acquired in patents for improvements. There was Eldred's brother-in-law, O. E. Cheesman, described by a contemporary as "perhaps a minor financial genius" and just possibly the man who sold Buehler the critical 10 shares of Victor stock.

It was decided at the meeting to make Cheesman general business manager with prime responsibility for sales of adding machines, rather than stock sales. Cheesman's salary: $5,000 a year. Optimistically, it was agreed that Cheesman's salary would escalate with rising sales and profits by $5,000 a year until he would be receiving $25,000 annually. Inventor Johantgen was designated engineer with prime responsibility for manufacturing.

And Carl Buehler was elected president, for two good and sufficient reasons. He was the only one among the directors and the small band of stockholders who was a bona fide businessman, experienced and successful, and he was the only one who had the money to give Victor Adding Machine Co. some badly needed infusions of new capital.

At the meeting he got to checking around with people on how they got into the company. He found that several of these people had done work for the company and had taken shares of stock instead of cash payments. Others were employed by firms that were doing work for the company and they had accepted shares, maybe a share a week or a month, for their pay. After everybody got acquainted, they all found out that Buehler was the only man in the group who had a business of any size, so they elected him president. He was supposed to be the angel. And they did make him a very attractive offer. If he would lend the company money, he would have the privilege of converting the notes into company stock at any time he desired.

Carl Buehler had just passed his 52nd birthday at the time of the 1918 annual meeting. He was the president and owner of a thriving business of his own. Yet, as the president and chief financial backer of Victor, he was in effect agreeing to a merger of elements—meat and office machines—that would make even the most merger-minded managers of today's "conglomerate" corporations hesitate. He not only knew nothing about the manufacture and sale of adding machines, he didn't as yet have one in his own business (although he was shortly to lay hands on five of the first machines to be turned out under his management of Victor). As a man who knew him well once said: "Carl's mechanical ability was such that he couldn't even hang a picture straight."

But he was a businessman of vision and, as his pioneering in building the meat market chain would indicate, he loved a business challenge. If he didn't have mechanical ability, if he knew little or nothing about manufacturing, he did have great and in-born talents as a merchandiser. Intuition and experience had given him a sure grasp of people, product, and price, and how they work together in the market place.

Thinking about his father, A.C. recalls that "Dad seemed to have the ability to reason out how things would work. He had a knowledge of people and their characteristics and their thinking. His basic premise was to try to satisfy the customer—to give good value at a low price. Businessmen didn't always think that way. The old idea was to sell a few products at a high price to the top of the economic pyramid. But Dad understood that the further down you go on the pyramid, the bigger the market; so if you could give a good value and get the price down very low, you were going to sell more. He'd do that in the meat markets by stocking the meats that were in good seasonal supply and, therefore, lower in price. In those days, the housewife with a hungry working family didn't demand fancy foods. What she wanted was good meat to fill up the family, and she knew she could get more for her dollar at Buehler Bros. than she could elsewhere. This is a phase of economics that Dad knew, and it carried over into Victor."

The products of the Victor Adding Machine Co. fit neatly with Buehler's business philosophy. Borrowing from the emerging techniques of mass production, inventor Johantgen had come up with a machine that was, theoretically at least, lighter, more compact, and less expensive than the models then being offered to the market. As the owner of a chain of small shops, Buehler knew at first hand that there was a market for a figuring machine at the right price.

Buehler also knew more than a little about employees—how to get them to work and work happily. You can read the same things today in a 700-page, polysyllabic book on labor-management relations, but Carl Buehler characteristically had it down to a few simple phrases: "Give a man a job to do, treat him with respect, recognize him when he does a good job, and let him make some money too."

But if Buehler had some confidence in himself and more than a little enthusiasm about the Victor product, he was also realistic. He had no intention of pouring money endlessly into Victor. He'd go to work at it, he'd give it a reasonable chance, and if it didn't pan out, he'd quit cold. That's what he told his chief lieutenant when he tapped him for the job.

CHAPTER 3

"You Make 'Em, I'll Sell 'Em"

Albert C. Buehler was 21 years old when his father first enlisted his help in running the affairs of the Victor Adding Machine Co. It was not the easiest time in the world for either Buehler, father or son. This was late in 1918 and Carl Buehler was advancing small but increasing amounts of money to keep the company afloat, while Johantgen, the inventor, and the others labored to perfect a machine for the market and to set up a working production line. Meanwhile, there was the Buehler Bros. chain to be managed. A.C. had been attending the University of Illinois College of Agriculture—and wondering about his future. There was always the question of his health after his history of childhood respiratory ailments.

For two reasons he had been enrolled in the agricultural college. There was the possibility that he would learn something that would be useful if he did enter the family meat business. Then there was his "insurance," as his father called it—some time before, his father had bought a farm on the outskirts of Chicago in what is now the luxury suburb of Barrington. A.C. spent summers there and the idea was that the outdoor life of a working gentleman farmer would be much more healthful for him than that of a businessman in the industrial city.

It might have been logical for Carl Buehler to keep his eldest son in the family's main and prospering business while assigning the second son, Herman or H.L., to the uncertainties of Victor Adding Machine. But, as A.C. recalls, "H.L. was fresh out of college and Dad felt there was a lot for him to *unlearn* before he could get down to being a businessman." A.C. was already well along in the unlearning or learning process. Then, too, A.C. had some credentials, vague as they might seem in retrospect, for working with machinery. On the farm he had tinkered with the equipment and had changed a spark plug on the truck and run the tractor. In that era of increasing fascination with the wonders of the internal combustion engine, A.C. was also an enthusiast of motor boat racing, working on the motors himself and driving in the races.

At first, A.C. worked at Victor only part time. From 6:30 in the morning onward, he'd work with his father at Buehler Bros. By 3:30 in the afternoon, the main business of the day would be over—the meat supplies purchased, the shipments on their way, most of the paperwork accomplished. Then one or both of the Buehlers would look in on the activities at Victor and start a second work day.

In the beginning, there was not much to see. The corporation consisted of two rooms in a building on Wells Street and shared space in another building at Washington and Green Streets in a section near Chicago's downtown Loop devoted to small machine shops and light manufacturing. Victor's own work force numbered barely half a dozen. They worked mainly as assemblers, putting together parts turned out by the neighboring machine shops.

But if the physical dimensions of Victor were small, the problems of the company were big and basic. One that seemed to overshadow the rest was this: Johantgen and his former associates had originally decided that it would be simpler and less costly to build a "nonlisting" adding machine. As the keys are depressed, and the handle pulled, dials move figures in front of a window much in the manner of the mileage device on an automobile; there was no "print-out." A nonlister eliminated the need for type, inked ribbon, paper roll, and the mechanisms for actuating all of these. With the nonlister, the clerk-operator simply copied off the totals and entered them in the proper records. But Victor was aiming at markets where the listing machine was standard. And Carl Buehler also had it in mind that Victor's specific market would be the shopkeeper and the small merchant. Both would want a ready record to see and keep or to hand to a customer.

There was a basic point of agreement and disagreement here. Up to the time of the Victor Adding Machine Co., adding machines had been big, cumbersome and expensive. They were sold only to business houses in the upper tiers of Buehler's marketing pyramid. What had attracted Buehler in the first place was the belief of Johantgen that he knew how to build a small and cheap machine, one that could be sold at the broad base of the pyramid. However, Buehler was not interested in a "cheap" machine; he wanted an inexpensive product, certainly, but he wanted value, too. As an early-day associate once said, "In the meat business,

Carl Buehler thought the way to make money was to take a small percentage of profit on a large volume. He made a fortune following that philosophy and naturally he carried it over into the adding machine business—a small percentage of profit on a product that has the quality and price to attract large sales."

The basic design of the original Victor machine—named the Victor 110—had a lot going for it. The inventors had perfected a simplified and compact mechanism. This meant among other things that the machine had only about 1,250 separate parts compared to 2,000 to 3,000 parts in the conventional machines of the day. It also meant a faster machine; the compact mechanism simply took less time to turn over, to record, to carry, to total and to print when the keys were depressed and the lever pulled. More importantly, from the manufacturing viewpoint, it was less expensive to build.

Further, having fewer parts, the tolerances of and between each part were less critical. Not that tolerance didn't remain highly important. The essential of any adding machine is that it must work accurately every time and all the time; if the mechanism produces a one cent error once in a thousand times, it is of no more use than if it never produced a correct figure or total. But obviously if only three parts are used to perform a function, the three need not be as finely made as 25 or 30 parts geared together to perform the same function. And, not at all incidentally, the possibility of mistake-producing wear is reduced.

The parts in the conventional machines of the day were cast and then milled to tolerance—a costly, two-step operation. Johantgen was able to use mass production screw machines and punch presses to turn out parts. At the same time, because the Victor needed fewer parts and did have a compact mechanism, the individual parts could be made out of stronger, thicker steel. All this added up to a final benefit: the Victor could be housed in a lightweight sheet

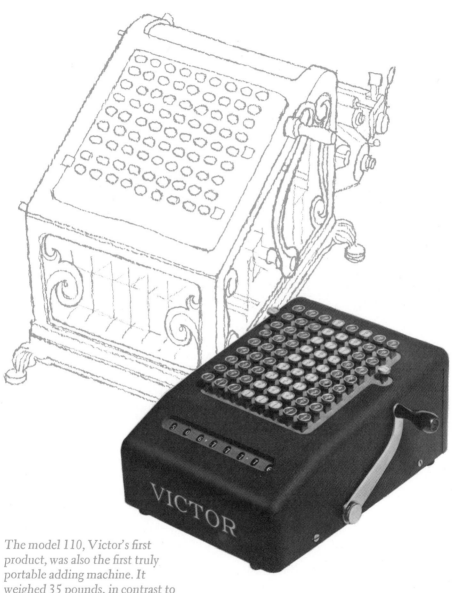

The model 110, Victor's first product, was also the first truly portable adding machine. It weighed 35 pounds, in contrast to standard machines of its day that weighed up to 100 pounds. This nonlister soon was followed by a machine with the same model number, but featuring a print-out tape.

metal cabinet instead of the cast iron housing used by the other manufacturers.

Victor had a true breakthrough. It was in fact coming up with a portable—the first portable—in an era when the standard machine was an outsize monstrosity. The standards weighed up to 100 pounds, and portability in the office could be achieved only by placing the machine in an iron pipe frame on casters. The Victor weighed only 35 pounds. Oddly enough, the early Victor salesmen did not attempt to exploit the "portable" feature; the term did not come into use in the field until half a dozen years later when the competition introduced even lighter machines to combat the Victor. It may seem strange that Victor did not sell the portable concept, but there was a good reason. The salesmen were kept busy combatting the idea, enthusiastically propagated by the competition, that the Victor was a "tin machine" that would, of course, fall apart in no time.

But, meanwhile, there were the many problems to be solved. Carl Buehler found out that he was in for some frustrating times.

With more humor than would have been possible then, A.C. now recalls the struggle:

"Dad would drop over to Victor with me and we'd get hold of the sales manager. Dad would ask: 'When are you fellows going to get some orders?' And the sales manager would say, 'I'll sell them when he makes them.' The man in charge of making them was Johantgen, so we'd go to Johantgen and Dad would ask, 'When are you going to make some machines?' And Johantgen would say, 'When he sells them, I'll make them.' It went on that way. 'How many are you going to sell?' 'How many are you going to make?' 'I'll sell all you can make.' 'I'll make all you can sell.' We weren't getting anywhere. At one point we brought in another general manager and put him in charge. As time went by, Dad would make suggestions on how to get things done. Then he'd go back and ask how it was going. 'Well, Mr. Buehler,' the answer would be, 'they tell me you don't do those things in the adding machine business.' So finally one day Dad said: 'Tell me, how long have you been in the adding machine business?' The answer was: 'Well, just since you put me here.' And Dad would ask about how long these fellows who were saying you don't do things that way had been in the business. It would be a foreman or an assembly man who had been on the job only a few weeks or months. Dad would say, 'They don't know any more about the adding machine business than I do, so how can they say my ideas are wrong?'

"They never did answer that, but they went on saying you don't do this or that in the adding machine business. After a few more times, Dad was a little bothered with the same old story and he finally said: 'You know, during the war we just finished over in Europe, when the army lost a battle, they didn't send 100,000 soldiers home and get another 100,000 soldiers. They'd get a new general, and that's what we're going to do.' So that fellow was on his way."

And A. C. Buehler was on *his* way, a very different way. At age 24, in 1921, A.C. became a full-time and permanent employee and officer of Victor Adding Machine Co.

CHAPTER 4

"A Couple of Pennies for Us"

The official minutes of the Victor Adding Machine Co. for the board meeting held on January 17, 1921, record without comment: "A. C. Buehler was elected vice president."

His father provided the comment, the advice and the marching orders. Much of what Carl Buehler had to say at the time strikes the ear today as homey philosophy rather than as a precise theory of business administration. But when he told his son to "go over there and see what you can do," he did lay down real and lasting guidelines that A.C. built on and added to and polished.

In a few short sentences, Carl Buehler told his son, among other things, how to run a family corporation and how to make it into something other than a family sinecure, the something other being what today's business writers might call a growth company.

As vividly recalled by A.C., here's what his father had to say:

"You know, we work hard over here in the meat business. We make some money so we can enjoy the good things in life. We spend it for whatever we want to spend it on. But here we are sending money over there to Victor every week and strangers are having the fun of spending our money. I think we ought to keep all the pleasures we can in the family. We make the money; let's have the fun of losing it, too, if that's the way it's going to be.

"But now I'll tell you, you go over there and every time a dollar comes in, you open up the drawer and drop in a couple of pennies—for us. Then you pay the bills and put the rest back into building the business.

"You work like the devil and get everybody else in the place to work like the devil. But you must remember that if you're going to get people to work with you, you've got to have a happy atmosphere. You've got to treat people right. Be nice to them and let them make some money too.

"Now go over there and look around and figure out how much money you need to pay your bills for six or eight months and let me know. I'll give you a check for that and then you get down to work and see what you can do. If we make some money, okay, we'll go on. If not, we'll quit."

Carl Buehler was willing to gamble, to put up risk capital, but in the last analysis, only if he could have control of it. He was willing to take a small profit for the family—the stockholders—but only if the balance of the profits were plowed into growth. He was willing to put money and time and work into a new product, but only so long as there was a chance for success. He was ready to face that toughest of all management decisions: to say, "All right, we've been wrong. We made a mistake. Let's cut our losses and get out."

A.C. looked into the costs, wages, materials, parts, assembly, shipping and sales. He gave his father a figure, got the check, and went to work.

In May, 1919, Carl Buehler made the big decision; he put Johantgen to work on a new version of the Model 110. The prime objective: to incorporate a print-out or listing capability. At the time, Burroughs and other manufacturers, established and just getting started, were offering a variety of adding machines. In the lower and medium range, there were five-column machines selling at about $250, and nine-column machines in the $300 to $400 range. At Victor, the initial agreement was that the company would bring out a seven-column machine.

But then somebody, "somebody who didn't know anything about adding machines," as A.C. recalls it, suggested that "we offer a little something extra by having a machine that would list seven digits, but total eight." That didn't make any sense to Johantgen. To give the machine an eight-digit totaling capability, it would be necessary to put in an extra adding wheel, adding rack, and type face—everything but the keys. So why not put in the keys and have an eight-column machine? Done. Victor would be selling a machine with a listing capacity greater than most of those in the lower and medium price brackets.

The machine was ready. But what of the Victor price? Carl Buehler studied A.C.'s cost figures briefly and made his decision without benefit of market surveys, market tests, cost accountants or any of the modern tools of management. One hundred dollars sounded to him like a "nice round figure" and $100 it was. This was August 15, 1921. The machine was the new and improved Model 110, eight banks, with tape, total and sub-total.

A.C. now knew what his job was: "to see if I could make them and sell them for $100 and have some money left over."

It had been a long and weary road for Oliver David Johantgen. Born in the tiny town of Oregon, Indiana, in 1875, Johantgen had been working on his "invention" since 1896. His first ideas for the adding machine came to him as he walked behind a plow on an Indiana farm, laying out geometric patterns and counting furrows.

He first translated his ideas into wood, whittling the parts out of old lumber.

Once Johantgen taught in a one-room school in rural Indiana for six months, but always the dream was with him. In 1899 he moved to Chicago and went to work as an apprentice in a metal working shop to get the experience he felt he needed to build a practical, working model in metal. Using the money he didn't need for food and lodging and working at nights and on Sundays, he succeeded in building the metal machine in late 1903. There was just one trouble with it, it didn't work. But it showed enough promise so that investors could see that it could be made to work. Actually, the papers Johantgen drew up for a 1903 patent application show that the machine contained many basics still in use in Victor machines today. It was a nonlister, but it used the 10-key principle, a keyboard that became popular only decades later. The early adding machines were full-keyboard; that is a key for each number from one to nine for each column of the keyboard.

As the years rolled by, Johantgen continued to tinker, to improve and to look for capital. He even managed one trip—unsuccessful—to Europe in an effort to promote a company. Finally, he found George Eldred in Chicago. Eldred agreed to put Johantgen on a small salary and to stand the expense of producing a working model in return for half interest in the patents. This was 1916. Johantgen was 41 years old. He spent the next 15 months perfecting the machine (still the nonlister, but a full-keyboard model) and tooling up for hoped-for production.

But by the time Johantgen was ready, Eldred was out of money. Still another year later, Eldred's brother-in-law, O. E. Cheesman, suggested a new start and the formation of Victor. As Johantgen recalled it, "He (Cheesman) proceeded to sell the stock while I supervised the mechanical work. The selling of stock seemed to be the hardest part, however, until we succeeded in adding Carl

Three inventors contributed
importantly to Victor's solid
growth. Oliver David Johantgen
(above) originated the 110,
Thomas O. Mehan (above right)
designed the 10-key adding
machine and the basic mechanism
for subsequent figuring machines,
and Oscar J. Sundstrand (right)
developed the automatic printing
calculator. Sundstrand still serves
as a Victor consultant.

Buehler to our list of stockholders. After that, our troubles were over as far as getting the necessary money was concerned."

However, the you-make-'em, I'll-sell-'em team of Johantgen and Cheesman succeeded in getting only a few of the nonlisters to market in 1919. And, as Johantgen said in an account written a decade later, "We soon came to the conclusion that there was a very limited field for this (nonlisting) machine, so in May of that year (1919) a meeting of the stockholders was held and a resolution passed to raise our capital stock to $200,000 in order to finance the listing model, which we started at once. We took a chance by making the additional tools required for the lister from my drawings without building a model. This was, of course, a rather desperate thing to do."

But the desperate gamble paid off, as Johantgen noted: "Our facilities for manufacturing at this time were very poor and we, therefore, had considerable trouble, both mechanical and financial. But as Mr. Buehler always came to our rescue with the necessary cash, we were finally able to overcome our mechanical troubles and began to make a little money about 1922."

A veteran Victor employee and foreman, now retired, John Kusinski, gives a little of the flavor of those early years: "Having been married at the tender age of 19 in 1919 and seeking to improve my earning power to meet my new obligations, I finally decided to seek a better paying job than the one I had at 45 cents an hour. At the end of March, 1920, I took a day off and happened to be passing number 817 West Washington Boulevard when I noticed a sign hanging outside which read, 'Help Wanted, Apply 6th Floor'. Taking the elevator to the sixth floor, I was immediately hired at 50 cents an hour. My first assignment was to rivet by hand many different-sized studs onto the main frame. Most of the components were made by Standard Tool & Die Works, also located on the sixth floor of the same building. The work force consisted of about ten men, plus A. C. Buehler, manager; Oliver Johantgen, the inventor, who also doubled as the final inspector; George Uhlig, the mechanical engineer; O. E. Cheesman, the sales force; and Christian Andersen, the shop foreman.

"After about six weeks, Mr. Andersen gave me an increase of five cents an hour and promoted me to the very interesting work of final adjuster. After a while, sales seemed to be going along pretty well, but suddenly Mr. Cheesman returned from his daily travels and notified Mr. Buehler that the competition had found a way to bring out a flaw in the operation of the Victor. The flaw: if you depressed all the nines across the top of the keyboard and then jerked the print handle, the machine would either lock up or print eights instead of nines.

"After testing a few of the 200 machines we had in stock, we found this was true and was caused by a lack of flexibility in the drive. At once Mr. Johantgen and Mr. Uhlig made design changes. Standard Tool and Die Works made sample parts, and when they proved to do the job of eliminating the flaw, we began to make parts by hand, filing them to the outline of the samples and having Standard Tool case harden them. This was done until dies could be made."

Perhaps it was a long haul for Oliver Johantgen; probably it appeared in 1919 and 1920 that the Victor Adding Machine Co. was a prime candidate for bankruptcy. But the larger truth was that, judged by usual corporate standards, the company was an overnight and resounding success. In just four years, Victor progressed from a company struggling to produce what appeared to be an unsalable item to one successfully producing a very acceptable machine. The official company records for 1922 give some indication of the success:

September 12: Special meeting of stockholders. Capital stock increased from 20,000 to 30,000 shares.

December 15: Special meeting of stockholders. Stock dividend of 15,000 shares, increasing capital stock to 45,000 shares.

Declared a five percent cash dividend equal to 50 cents per common share.

In the fifty-year history of Victor, the September 12, 1922, meeting of stockholders was as important as any. The stockholder vote formalized ownership and control of the company by the Buehler family. Par value of the Victor stock was $10, giving the 10,000 shares of new stock a value of $100,000. And Carl Buehler had put just that much into the company through loans and advances, in addition to his purchases of stock.

A letter from Carl Buehler was made a part of the record of the meeting: "It being a fact that the company is now indebted to me in the sum of $100,000 for actual cash advanced by me individually to maintain and develop its product and advance the sales thereof, I am willing to accept in full liquidation of this indebtedness 10,000 shares of common capital stock of the company . . ."

Having already purchased the 2,000 shares owned by O. E. Cheesman, who left the company in mid-1921, and having acquired the stock of various faint-hearted early investors, Carl Buehler held better than 50 percent of Victor's stock. Eventually his ownership reached more than 80 percent.

Buehler wasn't overly impressed with stock dividends. "You were just playing with pieces of paper," he said, "and your slice of the pie remained the same." But the fact is that Victor retained the $10-a-share par value on the increased shares and the pie itself was getting valuable.

Within a year of the introduction of the Model 110 at the $100 price, Victor had manufactured and sold 2,000 machines. And had a bonanza contract.

At least for Victor in 1922, it was a bonanza. The McCaskey Register Company of Alliance, Ohio marched in and signed a contract for 1,000 Victors with every indication that the minimum contract would be renewed annually. If McCaskey was a ten-strike for Victor, Victor was no less a godsend for McCaskey.

Founded in 1903 by P. A. McCaskey, the company had made a brilliant success out of what was essentially an early-day bookkeeping system for grocery and general store merchants. McCaskey had designed a carbon sales book and a revolving rack for orderly but handy storage of the books. When Mrs. Jones bought her groceries, the clerk would pick the proper book off the rack, add her day's purchases, note the new balance, hand Mrs. Jones the original and return the book to its place. But by the 1920s "cash and carry" was becoming more and more a factor and McCaskey's customers were looking for a means of keeping track of cash sales, a circumstance not overlooked by McCaskey's aggressive Ohio neighbor, the National Cash Register Co. of Dayton. McCaskey needed a cash register in its product line, but it had none of the necessary know-how to build its own and the registers on the market were, in the main, too expensive for the company's small merchant clientele. Victor, with its adding machine retailing at $100, offered an ideal solution. Put the adding machine on top of a cash drawer and you had an immediately desirable, inexpensive cash and record keeping unit. A second drawer, fitted with slots or leaves for holding McCaskey credit forms created another salable product.

"The first order for one thousand machines was really big business," A. C. Buehler recalls. "It was then probably the biggest single order ever placed for adding machines."

But McCaskey was not the whole of the story. Victor was rapidly building up a sales organization, first in Chicago, then in other major metropolitan areas. By late in 1921, the company had district sales managers at work in New York, Baltimore and Philadelphia. From the home office in Chicago, A. C. Buehler and a new general sales manager, F. B. Willis (hired at a salary of $416.66 a month, plus one percent of the cash derived from sales), ranged the Midwest and the East Coast lining up dealers.

The easiest way for Victor to build a selling force was to persuade established dealers to take on the line. Victor was not yet in the confident shape to take on a large standing payroll for salesmen and to sign contracts for branch office space. Usually the dealers could see the sales potential in a machine selling at $75 and more below competitive machines. The task was to convince them that the Victor was a quality machine—despite the unknown name on the label.

It was hard work and called for bright ideas, and even some fast talk on occasion. Sometimes A.C. spent weeks on the road, calling on dealers and later setting up branch offices and hiring salesmen. "In those days," he recalls, "we'd try to do our traveling at night to save time. If you worked the schedule right, you could see people until nine or ten at night and be in the next city for an eight o'clock meeting the next day. I'd even take a sleeper from New York to Philadelphia. They'd keep the Philadelphia car on a siding until seven o'clock in the morning. There were some advantages in the old days; you didn't have to bother with the time and fuss of getting into and out of a hotel and you didn't have to get up early in the morning to try to catch an airplane for the next city on the route. If you planned it right, you could cover a lot of towns and get a little rest, too."

One of the techniques developed was especially effective. A home office sales team would settle down in a city where Victor was unrepresented, hire four or five girls and put them to work on the telephone. The girls would call stores and business establishments and say they were making a survey of office equipment. Then they'd run through a questionnaire: how many typewriters, how many adding machines, how old were the machines, etc. The answers turned up a number of sales prospects: a business with an ancient adding machine, another with only one machine but of a size to make good use of two or three, a store still using the paper sack method of addition.

Then they would go to the dealer picked out and give him the sales campaign: how much national advertising was being done, their figures on the potential business in the town, and a sales talk about the Victor machine.

Finally, he was given a whole list of prospects with the names and addresses all laid out for him. He could see the chance to make some money. Then they would sell the dealer a bill of goods, a stock of machines. But it was a good bill of goods.

By 1923 some 400 dealers around the country were selling the Victor 110. In just a few years the total was 3,000.

If it hadn't been for the basic design of the machine and the manufacturing concept, growth on this order would have been difficult, if not impossible. As noted, the 110 was vastly less complex than competing machines. And although the parts were mass produced, they were precision stamped out of various thicknesses of low carbon sheet steel. They worked and continued to work. But when repairs were necessary, the job was often simple and easy.

Thus, Victor was largely spared the crushing cost of setting up a repair network—at least until the sheer number of machines in use made it inevitable that some machines would need service. A district sales manager in the early days of Victor once commented: "A dealer might have spent 10 to 15 years building up goodwill and a local reputation. When you consider that Victor was probably only a small percentage of his total store volume, he couldn't afford to tie himself up with a product that could cause as much grief as an adding machine that wasn't right. Our machine was right; you might say it had service built right into it."

Positive proof of that came in 1924. Victor sent each of its dealers a letter, taking note of the fact that selling adding machines was a new proposition for most of the dealers and saying that Victor was interested in knowing whether the dealer found the Victor franchise worthwhile. Then Victor made a bold offer. Any dealer who was dissatisfied could ship his machines back to the factory and the company would promptly write out a check for a full refund. The results were rather astounding. Not a single one of the machines came back.

Another sales manager remembers his days with the adding machine company for which he worked before joining Victor: "I always had a couple of calls to make every day to smooth over somebody who had had a lot of trouble with a machine. I found out that the best thing to do was to make the calls first thing in the morning and get it over with. But at Victor we would send the machines out and that would be the end of it."

A.C. has always been a man who sees a problem not as a barrier, but as a challenge. The lack of a service organization did create one problem for Victor. Initially, the company was locked out of the larger corporations. They demanded the protection of a service contract.

An early attempt to sell Wilson & Co. provides an example of the problem and the Victor reaction. The meat packing company was in the market for 95 machines, which would be placed in Wilson offices around the country. The direct competition was Burroughs, then the number one company in the field. Burroughs was offering a service guarantee at a flat annual fee. Victor sold Wilson on the idea that the Wilson offices could have a machine repaired locally and then apply to Victor for reimbursement. If repair costs ran more than $10 a machine annually, or more than $950 a year for the 95 machines, Victor would pay Wilson everything above those amounts. It turned out to be a good gamble for Victor. Wilson felt the agreement gave it adequate protection against service costs and bought the Victor machines. But the repair costs never did get any place near the $950 total. The plan was tried with a number of corporations with equal success. Ultimately, claims were so minor that all of the companies told Victor to forget about it, the bookkeeping bother was greater than the possible return.

Even the Victor, of course, could develop troubles. But even much later on, in the mid and late 1920s, when Victor had thousands of machines out in use and did set up its own service department, the need was minor in comparison to the competition's. At a time when some 15,000 Victors were in use in Manhattan, there were only three men in the company's service office. And A.C. complained that sometimes when he was in New York he'd see "all three just puttering around all day." But he conceded that the company should keep the three, not because of the volume of calls, but to assure prompt service in case the few calls were bunched. Victor's force of three gave it one serviceman for every 5,000 machines in use. The best of the competition at the time maintained one serviceman for every 1,000 machines in use.

Dating back to his part-time days at the company, A.C. had been Victor Employee Number Nine. Which is probably as good a way to identify him with the company as any. The duties of Employee Number Nine changed with the needs and the problems—production, sales, administration, finance. At one time or another he did everything, right down to operating a punch press. And his company title changed many times, too. In January of 1921 he had been designated vice president. Before mid-year he lost the vice presidential title and became the secretary-treasurer, to sign checks and other documents and to drop some pennies in the Buehler drawer, if possible. About the same time, his brother, H.L., became a member of the board of directors. (Of the five-man board, three were Buehlers: Carl, A.C. and H.L. One was a friend and legal adviser of Carl's. The fifth was Oliver Johantgen or, at various times, his insurance executive brother, J. F. Johantgen.)

But whatever his title, A.C. was into everything, a fact that inclines him to the school of thought that today argues for switching corporate managers from one department to another rather than hoping general managers and presidents will emerge through a single department.

Victor was making good, even spectacular, sales progress but there was, of course, the critical question of profits. Could Victor manufacture and profitably sell the 110 at Carl Buehler's good round figure of $100? As secretary-treasurer, A.C. totaled up the costs and did the accounting and evolved his continuing theory of pricing. Within reasonable limits, A.C. preferred to start with the market place when it came to pricing and work back to factory and materials costs. The heart of the matter: if you start with a survey of costs and total them to arrive at a price, everybody concerned tends to add in a comfortable margin for error. Imposing price on production creates a goal to shoot at, an incentive, as A.C. says, to "work like hell" to hold down costs and meet the target.

In sum, tight cost control and volume production translate into profits even with a low selling price. "Henry Ford proved it with the Model T," A.C. comments, "and it was really one of the first lessons I learned from Dad and our experience with the Model 110. Dad used Johantgen as an example. Suppose you invented an adding machine and whittled out all the parts yourself and built the machine and adjusted it and finally got a going piece of equipment. Even if you only valued yourself, your work, at $25 a week, you'd have to get about $20,000 for that one machine to stay alive. And an adding machine isn't worth $20,000 to anybody. The only answer is to get production, to get volume, on it. And production's got to have something to shoot for. If you let the boys out in production set their own price, they'll put a lot of cushion in it and they'll never admit that the overhead stays the same whether you're producing one or a thousand.

"You get the same tendency on the sales side. If you go to the lowest guy on the line and ask him for a sales forecast, he'll figure he should sell 10 machines, but he'll say eight to give himself a cushion. The local manager will take all the figures from his salesmen and cut the total down a little to give himself a cushion. So you work up through the district and regional managers and each one plays it a little on the safe side. It used to get up to me that way and I'd say, well, okay, boys, forget it, because with that little volume we can't afford to put it on the market. So we'd take the cushion out and set the figure still higher. It would work because everyone would have something to work at and he'd feel good at making progress."

If the company records for 1922 indicated that Victor was making progress, an entry in the minute books for one day of the year 1923 confirms that fact. The day was December 18 and the entry read: A cash dividend totaling $45,000 or $1 per share of stock, was declared by the board of directors. A stock dividend of 15,000 shares was also declared. The salary of A. C. Buehler, secretary and treasurer, was increased to $15,000 a year.

A.C. was 26 years old, he was making a handsome salary, he was deeply involved in the affairs of an exciting young company, and the great boom of the 1920s was under way. Obviously, the roaring prosperity of the period was a help to Victor; so too was the climate of change within the business community where old-fashioned ideas were being replaced by office machines and modern methods as quickly as the automobile was replacing the horse and buggy on the streets. But still it was the Victor concept— quality and merchandising—that counted. The company had made its first great strides against the sudden and sharp recession of 1921-22, which saw many companies, including some adding machine companies, go bankrupt or disappear in forced mergers.

Once the company got off the ground, growth itself created problems. There must have been times when Carl and A. C. Buehler felt they were in the real estate business. And someone must have been a minor genius at planning and logistics; otherwise, costs and chaos would have enveloped the company. As sales and production grew, Victor would rent more space. Then, when the maximum had been reached, a search for a new home would begin. Barely settled down, the company would feel the pinch of space and the process would begin again, as the early addresses indicate: South Wells Street, Green and Washington Streets, Carroll Street and Sacramento Avenue, Albany Avenue.

By 1924 management had wearied of the game. On October 1 the board of directors authorized the purchase of 100,000 square feet of land for $30,000 in Northwest Chicago. Three months later a general contractor, George Thomson & Co., was given a $112,000 contract to build a permanent home for Victor on the site. The original building is still standing and the address is the company's address today: 3900 North Rockwell Street.

The Buehlers had confidence in the future of the Victor Adding Machine Co. But the competition was starting to take some swings at Victor.

In 1924, six years after its founding, Victor purchased land (top) for the first building it was to own. The original structure (center) was completed in 1925. Facilities were expanded (lower) in 1942 for wartime production of the Norden bombsight. Sketched below are today's headquarters and main plant at 3900 North Rockwell Street, Chicago, Illinois, which include original building and all subsequent additions.

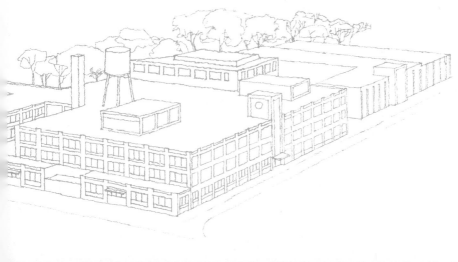

CHAPTER 5

Progress of Figuring Machines

Calculate, from the Latin, *calculus*, meaning pebble. The early Romans, and possibly their ancestors, the Etruscans, manipulated pebbles as a means of adding and subtracting with accuracy. From the dawn of civilization, man has sought an escape from the drudgery and mental gymnastics involved in doing arithmetic and in remembering or retaining the result. Without a doubt the fingers and the toes were the first mechanical aids: two fingers and two fingers, four: fold one finger, three. Hence the decimal system, counting based on tens, and the systems based on twenties used over the span of time by various peoples, including the ancient Aztecs and some present-day Eskimos.

Paradoxically, the more sophisticated process of addition has come more easily to some peoples than simple counting. Some primitive tribes in the remote corners of the world today (e.g., Australia, Ceylon) have words for only "one" and "two." "Three" becomes "two and one." Thus, the Biblical three score and ten (three times twenty, plus ten) was somehow easier for the Israelites than counting in higher numbers. Very early, the Romans went through one, two, three and four vertical lines to designate the numbers while adding the appropriate vertical lines to the five (V) for six, seven, eight and, again, nine. Then they advanced to the subtraction concept, using the single line in front of the V and in front of ten (X) for four and nine.

But always there was the need for the mechanical aid and the temporary or permanent recording device. Knots in strings were used as well as arrangements of pebbles. So too were scratch marks on walls, on clay tablets and, first of all, the ground. Many ancient civilizations "invented" the abacus or crude forms of this efficient but mentally demanding device for saving time and energy. It was known in China at least as long ago as 2637 B.C., but its name in the West derives from the Greek "*abak*," meaning "dust." Some scholars think the Greeks and Romans got the abacus from one or another of the Semitic cultures. Be that as it may, the Greek name doubtlessly indicates the ancestry of the device: a dust covered space or board on which a clerk could draw lines for the tens and hundreds and then make marks, wiping the board clean and starting over as needed.

In the long history of figuring there are many fascinating details. For instance, the Romans gave us our cumbersome inch and equally complicated ounce (both from the Latin *uncia*) in the attempt to set up units of trade (dozen, foot) that were easily divisible; e.g., 2, 3, 4, and 6 go into twelve.

A system of record-keeping used centuries later by the English provides another interesting footnote. For hundreds of years, and at least as late as the 17th century, financial transactions of one kind and another were recorded by cutting an appropriate number of notches in a stick. The wood piece was called a tally, from medieval French and the Latin meaning stick. When a two-sided transaction was involved, e.g., when a farm tenant borrowed from his lord and promised repayment, the stick would be appropriately notched on two sides, then split down the middle, providing two records that could be matched for agreement and honesty. Hence, the use of the noun and the verb today to mean an account or reckoning (a tally) and the balancing of accounts (to tally). Hence, also the modern stockholder, the descendent of the monied man who was a holder of tally sticks, or stocks, from the Anglo-Saxon stocc, meaning piece of wood or stick.

John Napier's rods or bones had no relationship to tally sticks and very little to the beads of an abacus. But this brilliant 17th-century Scot, like thousands of other men known and unknown over the course of history, was trying to reduce the tedium of mental computation. His bones or rods were rectangles inscribed with tables of numbers. Once the system was learned, the bones could be matched and appropriate numbers read off to short-cut complicated multiplication problems. If the bones, so called because the numerical tables were sometimes carved on bone, had a short and limited place in the history of figuring, not so another effort of Napier's at establishing the relationships of numbers. It was in 1614 that Napier published his revolutionary work on logarithms and thus, among other things, became the father of the engineer's slide rule.

Less than a decade later Blaise Pascal was born in France. While still a child, Pascal demonstrated his genius in theoretical mathematics, which gave his father, a well-to-do judge, an idea. Father turned over to his son the tedious job of keeping the family accounts and this very shortly gave his son an idea. At age 19, in 1642, Pascal invented an honest, workable computing machine. A series of numbered wheels, somewhat in the manner of a telephone dial, were geared in direct ratio to a corresponding series of numbered drums revolving past a slight opening at the top of the cabinet. "Dial" two on the wheel and the two would show in the opening. Dial two again and the drum would move two places to show four. Pascal also geared his drums so that the machine would carry; if the first drum on the right of the machine was moved through nine, a ratchet moved the next drum to the left to one. The direct gear and the carry transfer system used by Pascal is the foundation for almost all modern calculating machines. But the Pascal machine was cumbersome and slow and the technology of the times was not up to Pascal's inventive genius; handcrafting each part made the machine exorbitantly expensive. But, evidently, in view of Pascal's record as a philosopher and mathematician, the machine did serve that great function of all successful office machines since then: the freeing of humans from mind-drugging routine. And of the limited number of Pascal machines built, some were shown as mechanical marvels to royalty (e.g., to Louis XIV) and found their way into museums so that the Pascal machine is the first (or oldest) of all calculating machines to be preserved intact.

Before the century was out, another great mathematician and philosopher tried his hand at building a calculating machine. With somewhat similar results from the practical standpoint, Gottfried Wilhelm Liebnitz in 1694 demonstrated a machine that would add, subtract, divide, and multiply.

Over the centuries that followed, any number of scientists, back-

Man's earliest figuring machines included the abacus (top),
which traces to 2637 B.C.; Pascal's computing machine (center),
invented in 1642, the forerunner of all modern calculating machines;
and Liebnitz's calculating machine (below), produced in 1684.

room inventors and plain crackpots announced to an interested world that they had at last found the answer to man's age-old search for an easy and accurate way to compute. Many are noteworthy for major and minor contributions to the art.

One Liebnitz contemporary deserves mention not so much for the two experimental machines he produced, but for the statement he made in presenting the machines to England's Charles II. His adding machine, said inventor Samuel Morland, was "a new and most useful instrument for addition and subtraction of pounds, shillings, pence and farthings without charging the memory, disturbing the mind or exposing the operator to any uncertainty . . ."

But for one reason or another, ranging from design defects to lack of technology for manufacturing to pure inability to better the calculating speed of the human brain, figuring machines remained curiosities for longer than a century and a half after Liebnitz. And when practical adding machines did make their appearances, it was in the United States, not Europe, that the swiftest and most useful advances were made. In fact, within an amazingly short period of years during the great industrial boom that followed the Civil War, American inventive genius and American machine shops produced the basics of the modern office machine industry.

The great advance in the adding machine, beyond improvements in internal mechanical techniques, was the system that made the keyboard possible. Early machines presented the potential users with an immediate and obvious negative, a clumsy method of entering the figures to be added, e.g., the movement of a variety of wheels by hand or by a stylus. Patents were issued in Europe and the United States as early as 1850 and 1851 for keyboard machines.

But it was not until the late 1880s that the first truly practical and commercially successful adding machine appeared on the market. Dorr Eugene Felt, co-founder of Felt & Tarrant Manufacturing Company, inventor of the internationally famous "Comptometer," was granted his basic patent July 19, 1887, and that same year his company produced its first commercial machines, eight of them, all hand built. Serious manufacturing and sale of the Comptometer began in 1888.

Felt was also the inventor of the first practical recording-adding machine. He filed an application for a patent on it on January 11, 1888, and the patent was issued on June 11, 1889. The first of these machines, called the "Comptograph," was sold in 1889.

William Seward Burroughs, an ailing ex-bank clerk, inspired to seek a foolproof machine by years of fighting human error in bank accounting, was granted a patent in August, 1888 on a recording-adding machine. However, an improved machine based upon his patent was not produced until 1892 by his company, now the great Detroit-based Burroughs Corporation.

Felt & Tarrant and Burroughs, thirty years before Victor and many another company, pioneered and built the figuring machine industry, fighting inertia and the same kind of near-superstitious fear that today attaches to computerization and automation. But the years around 1880 initiated a practical revolution that continues today with the addition of such stars as Victor, IBM, SCM, and others. Looking back at the brief and explosive period, there was Felt's Comptometer and Comptograph, Burroughs' adding machine, C. L. Sholes' Remington typewriter No. 1 (1873), James and John Ritty's cash register (1877) for National Cash Register, A. B. Dick's mimeograph machine (1884), and Joseph Duncan's Addressograph system (1893).

Necessity may or may not be the true mother of invention, but in those days of the quick flowering of American business and industry, the need for something beyond the quill pen was there: in 1880, as a fair guess, 172,000 office workers were employed in

American business; ten years later, the total was 801,455, according to U.S. Census Bureau figures.

But the invention and manufacture of functioning machines to meet a real need was not the end of the story. There was the matter of selling, of getting the machine to the place where it could be put to use. In the beginning, it wasn't at all easy.

J. A. V. Turck, an engineer and a student of machine calculating, writing in his book, *Origin of Modern Calculating Machines*, published in 1921 by the Western Society of Engineers, pointed up the problem in these words:

"In the early days when the key-driven calculator was marketed, and later when the recording adder was also placed on the market, the efforts of the salesmen for each of these types of machines . . . were met with anything but enthusiasm. Of course, now and then a wide-awake businessman was willing to be shown and would purchase, but ninety-nine out of the hundred who really had use for a machine of either type could not at that early date be awakened to the fact . . .

"It was strongly evident that the efforts of bookkeepers and counting house clerks to prevent these machines entering their department were inspired by the fear that it would displace their services and interfere with their chances of a livelihood . . .

"This class and even those in charge of large departments took the mere suggestion that they had use for a calculator or a recording adder as an insult to efficiency and would almost throw the salesman out."

In the few cases when fear was not paramount, an equally unhelpful attitude was apparent. The machines were thought of as mechanical tricks, in the sleight-of-hand magic category. A supposed salesman for one pioneer company did much better than his colleagues for a while. He put his sample machine in a wheelbarrow and trundled it from bar to bar, making bets on the machine's ability to come up with the correct answers to lengthy problems.

When Victor began selling in the early 1920s, its problems were of a different order. Mainly, they had to do with achieving distribution and with convincing the buying public that the compact, inexpensive "adding machine for everyone" was reliable even though the Victor name was relatively unknown. Boldly, the company began to advertise nationally in 1923. It placed a four-color advertisement in the *Saturday Evening Post* to announce the new, improved Model 310. (The art work on the advertisement was done by a very young man who later became famous for his work on figures of another kind. This was George Petty of *Esquire* and *Playboy* fame.)

At the same time, selling techniques were being refined. By 1923, Victor had its own magazine aimed at providing information and inspiration for the salesmen. It was (and still is) called *Walk and Talk*, a reflection of the Buehler belief that the way to sell an office machine is to get out on the street, talk to every possible prospect and demonstrate the machine in the customer's office. All this was made possible by the Victor machine's light, easy-to-carry weight. The November 15, 1923, issue of *Walk and Talk* reported that a special crew of Victor salesmen had turned the city of Chicago into a sales laboratory. For several months, every sales technique from telephone to cold canvass had been tried and the results meticulously noted. Out of the tests came a standard selling method: "short, quick, snappy sales demonstrations and trials." A "One Minute Standard Approach," which eliminated "all useless conversation," was commended to Victor salesmen henceforth. The One Minute Standard Approach:

"My name is ———— ————. I sell the Victor adding machine. No doubt you have seen it advertised in the *Saturday Evening Post* and other publications. The Victor is that wonderful machine which is standard in every respect. It does all kinds of adding, calculating and tabulating, and sells for the remarkably low price of $100. We have sold over 35,000 of them to all classes of business, large and small. They are used by the Standard Oil Company, International Harvester, railroads and other large corporations. We can save you in actual cash $500 or more by making every figuring and bookkeeping operation in your business 100 percent accurate. I know you're a busy man and I do not want to take up any more of your time now. I merely want your permission to show you this machine."

If the standard approach was a little on the boastful side when it sought to leave the impression that the Victor was the favorite of the largest corporations and when it claimed the machine could do "all kinds" of calculating and tabulating, the essence of the message was everything that it should have been.

For a very small outlay, the businessman and shopkeeper could buy money-saving accuracy. As A. C. Buehler once put it:

"We sold accuracy insurance in those days on a very inexpensive term basis. Our early literature even looked like an insurance policy. We'd often sell the machine on the installment plan and we'd show the fellow how he was buying a year's worth of accuracy insurance for about 3½ cents a day. Figuring 25 working days a month in those days, that would come out to about $100 purchase price over the life of the machine. We'd go in and ask the man to give us the bills he had sent his customers and the bills he had paid his suppliers. We'd run through them on the Victor and every time we'd find mistakes. We'd point out to him that every mistake he made in favor of the customer was money out of the window and every mistake he made in his favor ran him the risk of losing an angry customer. With his suppliers, he was usually spending money he didn't owe. We were betting he had made mistakes and we usually won."

"Walk and Talk, the Secret of Successful Selling," summarized Victor's basic sales philosophy from the beginning. Shown are 1923 and 1968 issues of "Walk and Talk" magazine aimed at providing information and inspiration for the salesmen.

Once the Victor machine almost crossed up A.C. on a very important sale. A.C. had an introduction to Clarence Saunders, one of the great, flamboyant entrepreneurs of the 1920s and the founder of the Piggly-Wiggly grocery store chain. A.C. was to meet Saunders in his Memphis, Tennessee headquarters. It was the dead of winter when A.C.'s train arrived in Memphis very early in the morning with the temperature unseasonably low. Some time later, A.C. was demonstrating the glories of the Victor machine to Saunders. But to his horror, the machine wouldn't produce a correct total! Perspiring and working like mad, A.C. had quickly realized what the trouble was. He had handed over his demonstration machine to a porter at the railway station. And the porter had left the machine standing on the freezing open plat-form of the train overnight.

An early problem with adding machines had been this: unless the totaling handle was pulled at a deliberate speed, one of the drums producing the figures in the total might stop too soon (when the pull was half-hearted) or roll past the correct figure (when the handle was jerked). To correct this, to produce an even pull on the internal mechanism, the machines were equipped with a governor. The governor was an oil-filled cylinder. In the cold of the platform, the oil in A.C.'s machine had become stiff, throw-ing off the action of the machine. To keep Saunders from getting a good look at the tapes, A.C. quickly crumpled them up as he tore them off the machine and threw them into a wastebasket. A.C.'s sales pitch proved successful and Saunders agreed to an impressive purchase, 100 machines. But A.C. was terrified at the possibility that someone would rummage through the tapes and spot all the errors. He could see a telegram of cancellation arriving in Chicago about the same time that he did. Obviously, A.C. couldn't walk off with the wastebasket or with its contents. Calmly, he lighted a match for his cigarette and dropped the lighted match into the wastebasket. A.C. made a great display of scrambling to put the fire out and of apologizing for such a "silly" thing. Years later, A.C. confessed to Saunders and Saunders, appreciating the predicament A.C. had been in, remarked: "You know, I think I would have bought the machines anyway, even if you hadn't burned the tapes and even if I had found you out, just because you were smart enough to fool me in the first place."

Victor was rolling along doing about $1,000,000 a year in sales in the early twenties when Burroughs and other competitors began to realize that the Victor men, "walking and talking" and carrying their lightweight machines instead of mere pictures into the stores and offices, were taking a sizable bite of the market. Not only was Victor getting some of the corporate business the other companies had been enjoying, but it was also making an eye-opening entry into the small business market, largely neglected by the established makers or poorly served by companies with inadequate machines. Often, according to one contemporary account, "Competitors were astonished to find Victor machines appearing everywhere, even in the little shop next door to their own office... whom they had never considered a potential customer."

The response of the rivals in the industry was to bring out portables. Or at least to introduce smaller models that were talked about and advertised as portables even though they were only less weighty versions of the standard models. (True portables, designed from the ground up as portables and including features of the standards, were a decade or more away and Victor would introduce them when they did come out.) At the time, the industry offered all of its models with odd-column keyboards. That is, everyone except Victor. Victor's one and only model, the improved 310, had eight columns of keys across and could show an eight-figure total. At $100 it was competing against more expensive machines that offered only seven column keyboards. This gave Victor an easily and obviously exploitable sales advantage.

In 1925 Victor moved to 3900 North Rockwell, still the address of Victor headquarters and of the main plant—its first company-built and company-owned factory. The company, having been able to apply mass-production techniques to a handcraft industry, was now able in its new home plant to put production on an even more efficient basis.

A Victor ad in the *Saturday Evening Post* early in 1925 bragged that "nearly 100,000" Victor machines were in use. At retail, almost $10,000,000 worth of Victor machines had been sold in four years, a noteworthy record, particularly in view of the size of the market and the size of the economy in that day.

If the competition was shooting at Victor, it couldn't be said that the war was effective. The company's sales (principally to dealers) for the full year of 1925 amounted to $1,902,000, almost nine times what they were in 1921.

So far Victor had made most of the right moves, but, like all aggressive companies, it did make mistakes.

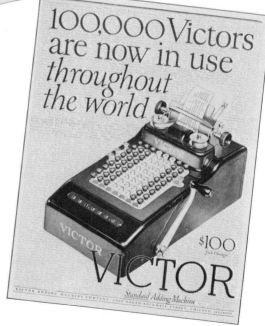

Victor heralded the approach and arrival of its 100,000th figuring machine with full-page ads in the "Saturday Evening Post" in 1925 and 1926. Latter ad was remarkably modern even by today's standards in its use of illustration and brief, hard-hitting text.

CHAPTER 6

Adding Machines + Bombsights

Looking back over a full 50 years of Victor history and his own role in the active management of the company for almost as many years, A. C. Buehler is moved to tip his hat gratefully in the direction of Lady Luck. But luck is seldom more than a contributing factor in success. Certainly, before luck, good or bad, can play a part, a decision must be taken and a venture launched. Despite what he might say, A.C. was never one to sit on the fence and wait for providence to show the way.

"I guess," A.C. says, "I've never been afraid to take a chance. In fact, you'd have to say that in business you've just got to take chances. Sometimes you go wrong, of course. But you just have to keep trying, that's all. I only know one way and that is to make a decision and then really to work and try to make it succeed. I figure if you're 60 to 70 percent right, then you're doing about as well as anyone can expect. Then you only have 30 to 40 percent to change. That's when you take a new look, adjust your thinking, and go to work correcting your mistakes."

From the official minutes of Victor board of directors meetings held during 1925:

A cash dividend equal to 50 cents a share on the 60,000 shares of common stock then outstanding is approved.

The salary of A. C. Buehler, secretary of the corporation, is raised from $15,000 to $18,000 a year.

In 1925, the directors decided that the secretary should enter into negotiations to purchase from the Simmons Boat Company the property immediately north of the Victor building for $40,000 or less for future expansion.

Directors, including Carl Buehler, A. C. Buehler, and H. L. Buehler, proposed an increase in the common stock to 100,000 shares and a new issue of 10,000 shares of six percent cumulative preferred stock, the preferred to be used to reward key employees.

Directors agreed to give an inventor and businessman, Max Garbell, 2,000 shares of the preferred stock in return for his patents on a portable typewriter, to put Garbell on the payroll at an annual salary of $5,000, and to pay Garbell a bonus of 25 cents on each typewriter manufactured up to 50 a day, 20 cents for each one manufactured from 50 to 100 a day and 15 cents for all thereafter. A. C. Buehler was instructed to assist Garbell in the completion of a first model and the company agreed to pay all developmental expense on the project.

The Garbell typewriter looked like instant success for Victor, perhaps even a repeat of the success story of the Victor adding machine. As a portable, it was lightweight and compact. The inventor felt it could be successfully marketed with a very low price tag—$60. In addition, the typewriter would give Victor product diversification, but would not put unusual strain on the company's talents in administration, production, or sales. Victor certainly knew how to produce small precision parts and to assemble a precision keyboard machine. In part, at least, Victor's salesmen and dealers would be selling the typewriter to their regular office equipment customers.

But somehow the Garbell typewriter didn't quite get off the ground. One immediate snag on the business side was quickly cleared up. Earlier, a Victor Typewriter Company of Scranton, Pennsylvania, had sold a typewriter and had called it the Victor. A.C. succeeded in buying the name and the goodwill from Victor Typewriter Company for $15,000—$5,000 less than the maximum authorized by the Victor board. But the rest of the history of the Garbell typewriter doubtlessly would have a discouragingly familiar ring if retold to any modern day new product manager. First there was a lengthy history of developmental work and expense. Once out of the laboratory and into the shop, the typewriter showed a dismaying tendency to develop bugs. The design was revolutionary because the shift worked on a rocker basis rather than the conventional up-down principle. Victor did succeed in producing and selling a few of the portables, but by then the calendar read 1929. Shortly thereafter the economics of the day provided utterly no reason to take a chance on a troublesome new product.

However, in the main, the Victor Adding Machine Co. reached its 10th anniversary year in 1928 in good and promising shape despite what economists would later see as the beginnings of a business tendency toward belt-tightening and despite fierce competitive conditions.

To maintain Victor's position in the face of that competition, the board had given approval in the spring of 1926 for the manufacture of a six-column adding machine to be priced at $75. Victor's changing product mixed with reduced prices meant that total unit sales were maintained or even increased. But the company's dollar volume did not benefit. Carl Buehler reported the 1928 results to stockholders:

Unit sales showed an increase of 27 percent over 1927. But dollar volume at $1,710,000 was actually under the 1925 level. Nevertheless, efficient Victor managed to produce a 24 percent increase in profits (before the minimal taxes of that year). Pre-tax earnings were $193,000.

This was the year—1928—that A.C. got the $125,000 shotgun. His father and others in the family used to kid him about owning the world's most expensive shotgun. But it was a rare bargain at the price.

In the mid-1920s, an old-time inventor named William S. Gubelman had succeeded in establishing his rights under a series of broad adding machine patents. Various adding machine companies were negotiating with Gubelman when Remington Cash Register Company, Inc. settled its own case by buying the full rights to the Gubelman patents. In turn, Remington sought to recoup by going after the other companies in the industry.

There had been some multimillion dollar settlements by the time the Remington legal department got around to serving notice on Victor. A.C., always the board's man when a trouble-shooter was needed, was given the task of negotiating with Remington. Figuring out his approach well in advance, A.C. went straight to the president. A.C. pleaded for a "good, low bridge deal" that would be easy on Victor, but make money in the long run for

VICTOR "Six"
Standard Adding Machine

The Above Full Page Advertisement Appears in the
Saturday Evening Post
October 23, 1926

The Victor "Six," a smaller six-column capacity version of the well-established Victor "Eight," was introduced at $75 in 1926 with this full-page "Saturday Evening Post" ad that offered a free trial and easy payments. A later version of this model featuring subtraction is shown in use.

Remington. Here was the logic: Remington had made flat, lump settlements with the other companies. Hence, Remington would get nothing more out of the patents from the balance of the industry. But yet there was a way. Victor and Remington could settle for a small, lump sum plus a royalty agreement on future sales. Victor, utilizing the Gubelman patents and undamaged by a big patent settlement, would go out and take business away from the competition. And Remington would collect on each machine sold.

It sounded fine to Remington. The terms were settled: a flat payment of $125,000 and a two percent royalty on all sales over $3,000,000 a year for the life of the Gubelman patents. Pleased, Remington dispatched an expert from its arms division to Chicago to take A.C.'s measurements and then made A.C. a present of a beautiful 20-gauge, custom-made shotgun. But it was the disarming young man from the midwest who took Remington's measure. No one at Remington, then a multimillion dollar corporation, had bothered to ask to see the books of the Buehler-owned corporation. The Remington people were flabbergasted, to say the least, when they did learn that Victor was more than a million dollars shy of the needed sales. The patents ran out before Victor ever did have to pay Remington more than a few thousand dollars in royalties, but they could hardly believe that Victor was not doing $3,000,000. They had all these reports from the field that Victor was beating the competition's ears back. But they were sportsmen; they recognized they'd made a deal and they stuck by it.

As good as the deal was for Victor, the unforeseen disappearance of $125,000 in one year was not a welcome event. This, and the typical Buehler reaction to it, may account for a certain undertone to the established family joke about the $125,000 shotgun.

Any family-owned corporation is always subject to the charge that the company's future may be compromised by selfish family thinking and immediate financial needs. But Carl Buehler and his sons took the broad view: the future of the corporation was what counted. Accordingly, in January of 1929, cash dividends for the common stockholders were temporarily suspended with these notations in the minutes of the board of directors meeting:

"Cash position was greatly handicapped during the year not only by expense involved in connection with the subtractor models, but also by the necessity of a payment amounting to $125,000 for the settlement of past infringement and future license on the Gubelman patents. The company witnessed a very trying year during 1928. The competition was very keen and it was necessary to make many changes. The personnel of our sales force was changed with just a few exceptions. Successful representatives were promoted to better positions and new blood was added in the form of the employment of experienced men of other companies. The results are shown by the fact that 32 percent of sales and 44 percent of profits for the year were obtained during the last quarter."

Early in 1928, when the weakness had begun to show in sales, A.C. had been given full and direct responsibility for the sales department. Now he was told to give the same personal attention to the production line where the two tenth anniversary models were not moving on schedule.

For the first ten years of its corporate life, Victor had built its success on a high-quality, low-cost straight adding machine. But, if the future were to match the past, Victor had to seek new markets with new and improved products. Announced in 1928 were the Model 310S and the Model 320S—"S" for subtraction. The first of the new models was, of course, Victor's famous 310 eight-column adder, improved to offer the customer the subtraction function. The 320S was a larger machine with ten-column capacity in both addition and subtraction.

In the March 20, 1928 edition of its sales publication, *Walk and Talk*, Victor exhorted its salesmen to new efforts: "With the coming of Victor's new machines, especially the new heavy-duty, 10-column machine with direct subtraction, a new and tremendously large field is opened up for the sale of adding machines by the Victor organization. Where, heretofore, Victor representatives have had to be content with selling our Model 310 machine for work not to exceed the capacity of one million dollars, the new Model 320S will enable you to meet the demand of those customers for a larger capacity machine, where an adding capacity of one hundred million dollars is necessary . . . With the new 10-column standard Victor machine, with direct subtraction, at the price of $125, Victor representatives should concentrate their efforts on big businesses . . . Tell your Victor message to the banks and other large concerns; give them, as well as the small grocery, the chance to buy the value that Victor offers."

Meanwhile, other important improvements were on the way: different carriage sizes to hold differing widths of paper tape, machines fitted to compute English currency, or 1/8 and 1/12 fractions, or hours and minutes or feet and inches. What the company called its "inventive experimental" department, under Johantgen's direction, was separated from the production department and given an impressive, for the company and the times, budget of $150,000. One assignment: to design a machine equipped with an electric motor drive. A separate department was established to handle day-to-day engineering problems on the production line.

As the work on the English currency machine might indicate, Victor had been a surprisingly early and successful exporter. By the late twenties, foreign business was strong enough to warrant an overseas advertising campaign. (In early 1929 directors voted to set up as a reserve for foreign advertising two percent of foreign sales.) On January 19, 1929, Evan Hansard, manager of export sales, took off on a trip to the West Indies, Cuba and Latin America to sign up additional Victor sales representatives. And Alvin Bakewell, the young assistant export manager at the time, confidently predicted that 1929 export sales would show a 50 percent gain over 1928 volume.

And it was true that in the years ahead incidental export sales were a real benefit to Victor as it struggled along with the rest of industry to stay afloat during the Great Depression.

Once, as a young man, A. C. Buehler had proposed a forthright plan for strengthening the position of a Buehler Bros. meat market located in a small Michigan city. The plan: cut prices to the bone, grab the lion's share of trade, drive the competition out of business. His father demurred: price cutting only for the sake of price cutting is bad business practice. It weakens the company for the long haul and in the end creates customer ill will in that some day prices must be restored to a level that will produce reasonable profits. Price reductions based on sound business savings are healthy. On the other hand, price cutting based on a determination to drive another business under is not only unhealtny but dangerous. There'll always be someone willing to jump in. If you do drive the other business under, someone will buy the fixtures and assets at fire sale prices and be in a position to offer even tougher competition. When A.C. asked him what the solution was, Carl Buehler replied, "If you have any right to stay in business, you must compete effectively and make a profit, too. Anyone can *lose* money."

The lesson stayed with A.C. and, as was often the case, it was interpreted and applied years later. Thus in October of 1931, in a basic policy statement, A.C. wrote:

"The general trend of present-day prices is downward. Price cutting is rapidly becoming prevalent as one of the methods of meeting competition and creating demand. A definite line may be drawn between the two most prevalent means of general merchandising today. One alternative is to offer the same product at lower prices, the other an improved product at the standard list price. The radio industry is a very good example of price cutting by offering the same product at a lower price. The automobile industry presents the workings of the other plan—offering a better product at the standard price.

"We recall the old Model T Ford at the time of its inception and make a comparison with it and the new Model A sedan. Of course, there is no comparison. Yet both have been sold for approximately the same price.

"The Victor Adding Machine Co., after consideration of both plans, has definitely decided to adhere to past policies, manufacturing the best and greatest dollar-for-dollar value in adding machines today."

By the end of that year, in line with the policy decision, Victor announced two new models, the 511S-12 and the 521S-12, both direct descendants of earlier Victor eight- and ten-column machines, both vast improvements on those earlier models, both powered by electric motors, both firsts in the industry at their price.

Progressive and strong management helped Victor through the depths of the Great Depression. But nothing any management could do accomplished much more than an alleviation of the general disaster. When he addressed the annual meeting of stockholders on January 20, 1931, Carl Buehler could find little to support his natural optimism. His remarks give a bleak but accurate flavor of the times:

"We, along with others, have suffered from the general depression which is still upon us. Our general experience has been that most concerns have set their foot down on purchasing new equipment. Many instances have also been called to our attention wherein consolidations have left the (surviving) companies with a surplus stock of office equipment. Our men, in their efforts to

In late 1931, during the Great
Depression, Victor introduced the
511S-12 eight-column (shown above)
and 521S-12 ten-column electric
calculating machines, both firsts in
the industry at their price.

create sales, either have been turned down or forced to make unprofitable allowances to get business. Where surplus equipment
was disposed of, it found its way to the secondhand market and
increased competition for what little business was available.

"Domestic sales this year are 30 percent lower than 1929. This
decrease was general throughout the United States and resulted
in an increase in sales cost of about 10 percent. Costs have been
gradually reduced to a minimum, but it has been necessary for us
to maintain at least a skeleton organization to serve our present
users and handle the few orders coming through from national
accounts who have purchased from us for years. In most cases, even
a skeleton organization is unprofitable, but it is necessary that we
serve our users in bad times if we are to enjoy the profit from their
purchases in good times . . .

"The McCaskey Register Company has always been a profitable
account. During 1930 their volume slumped to the lowest point
in (Victor) history. Not one order has been received from them
since last August.

"Exports have suffered in addition to the others. The present
tariff has been a great handicap. Foreign countries are reluctant
to do anything until they see how it works out . . . Nevertheless,
in spite of our reduction in export sales we show a two percent increase in participation (in total exports of adding machines) over
the previous year. Apparently, other companies have suffered to a
greater extent than we have. Late in the year, on the introduction
of our machines for handling British currency, we gathered new
hope. Sales to Great Britain are beginning to come in . . .

"Manufacturing costs, due to the low volume, have increased
seven percent. Cuts have been made in labor rates, as well as those
of the foremen. In fact, all manufacturing costs have been cut to
the bone.

"Our factory is now operating on a 60 percent lower basis than one year ago. Its schedule is running slightly lower than the number of machines sold and our inventory is being reduced to make up this difference. . .

"Clerical and office expenses have also been reduced, not only in the number of employees, but in salaries as well. . .

"Earnings for the year 1930 will run about 33 cents per share. (Note: This meant dollar profits of about $33,000.) Inventories have been reduced in proportion to sales. Current ratio of assets to liabilities is 3½ to 1 as compared to 3 to 1 last year, more evidence of the basically strong position of your company. . .

"The prospects for the coming year are difficult to forecast. Adding machines are not vitally essential for the average business. At least, new equipment is not necessary until expansion programs are put into effect. And then only until such plans are well under way can we hope for much improvement. In the meantime, we will sit tight, cut expenses wherever possible, and wait for business to revive."

A year later, on January 18, 1932, when Buehler reported to his fellow stockholders, conditions were even worse. For the first time since the early development days, the company was losing money. But the nature of the disaster had been assessed realistically and Victor had done something more than sit and wait. Perhaps the new line of electrics would spark a sales revival.

Bluntly, Buehler reported: "Sales for 1931 are less, by 50 percent, when compared with the previous year . . . Throughout the summer and fall months, we offered prizes and special discounts as an inducement to accelerate business. The results were not only disappointing, but expensive because they failed to increase sales to any noticeable extent. We have no way of comparing our loss of volume with that of other adding machine companies, but we feel that we have held our position in the industry. One concern, to our knowledge, has reduced its sales force 60 percent, two others are practically out of business, and another is being offered for sale . . .

"In general, all salaries were cut from 10 to 20 percent and, in many cases, personnel eliminated . . . (But) operations for the year resulted in a loss of $29,000 . . . What the future holds is too hazardous to predict. But our line which includes right-hand control and electric models should help a good deal. Just a small increase in sales with our present low overhead will put us on the right side of the ledger. We are neither hopeful, nor expectant, because we do realize we are up against hard times.

"With the facts before us, we enter the new year with determination—a slight break in our favor should result in a much improved showing."

Reporting formally as president of the corporation on Victor's affairs, Buehler spoke with hardheaded business sense of his efforts to cut expenses by trimming employment and cutting wages and salaries. But a first tenet of his personal business philosophy had always been the fairest possible treatment of employees, and through the years of the depression Victor strove to minimize the impact of the depression on Victor workers. A determined effort was made to give each employee as much work as possible, an hour to a full work week. And to rehire whenever feasible.

A former employee, now retired, recalls: "At times during the depression, Victor worked four-hour days and five-day weeks instead of the standard five and one-half days. They tried their best for us. The works manager himself used to come over to our home with his car and pick me up just so I'd be able to get in a few hours of work. They'd also send people around to the homes to find out if people needed any help. If we had debts, they'd help you figure out a way to pay them off and they'd pay them off too. Then you repaid the company whenever you were able to. At work, soup and coffee were served free to the employees and they set up a way we could buy Buehler Bros. meat at the plant at wholesale prices."

In addition, food baskets and coal for heating were sent to any number of homes of employees and, in good times and bad, physicians and specialists were sent when needed and the bills paid by the Buehlers. Another retired employee comments: "Victor's policy of trying to keep going and trying to keep people together and help people during the depression was important to me and to my co-workers and the result was that Victor hit World War II with a good staff of capable and loyal help."

For Victor and for the Buehler family, 1932 was the blackest of years. In failing health, Carl Buehler died on October 26, 1932. He was 66 years old. His death left Victor in control of his widow, the energetic and strong-minded Mrs. Rose Buehler, and his four competitive sons. At the time A.C. was 35 years old and had been both a director and officer (vice president or secretary-treasurer) since 1921. The second son, Herman L., was two years younger, had been elected a director a few months after A.C. in 1921, but had devoted his major energies to the family meat business, finally going on the roll at Victor as assistant secretary-treasurer in 1927. This was the same year that the third son, Robert O., was made secretary-treasurer. Born in April, 1903, R.O. was 29 at the time of his father's death and had vigorously and effectively taken up his father's civic, church and boys' club work. For many years R.O., at his own expense, has devoted his time and energy to boys' club work and other public service. He is now Mayor of the City of Galena, Illinois. The fourth and youngest son, C.C., was only 25 in 1932. The most well-endowed of the four, according to his older brothers, he was to die an early death in 1964. He had become a director and an assistant secretary-treasurer in 1936.

At the annual meeting of stockholders in January of 1933, A.C. was elected president with R.O. remaining as secretary-treasurer. The board consisted of A.C., H.L., R.O. and two operating men, the sales and production managers. As president, A.C. cut his already reduced salary down to $8,775, less than half his 1925 salary of $18,000. The following year he cut himself again to $8,100.

The times were uncertain enough without the loss of the wise head of Carl Buehler, but Victor managed to move ahead through the 1930s even though the four brothers often found it hard to agree on solutions for the day's problems. Then, too, there was Buehler Bros. to be managed, a task undertaken by H.L. with the help of C.C. A succession of general managers, sales managers and production managers moved in—and out—of Victor as the brothers sought unsuccessfully to add an unspecified ingredient to top management.

The slow but real revival of the national economy through the mid-thirties helped the struggling company. Addressing the stockholders meeting in January of 1936, A.C. took note of Victor's progress:

"We have expanded in sales and production and our organization . . . is, perhaps, in better condition than for some time in the past, due principally to the development of men who have been with us for some years. . . .

"Sales for the year 1935 exceeded sales of 1934 by 39 percent. Domestic sales increased 56 percent, negotiated sales by 97 percent, while export sales decreased 10 percent. The decrease in export sales was anticipated in view of the many complications arising in the conduct of export business under present-day circumstances. . . .

"Manufacturing efficiency was increased . . . with low operating costs prevailing and with steady employment for all factory forces.

"Net operating profit, before federal income tax, amounted to $89,000 as compared with $41,000 in the previous year. After federal income tax, there remained a net profit of $76,000 as compared with $34,000. This is an increase of 122 percent. When considering that sales expanded 39 percent and net income 122 percent, it should be evident that we have been operating efficiently...

"As of the close of the year, for each dollar of liability, the company had available $7.78 in good current assets. A review of the history of the company indicates a sounder current position at the close of 1935 than at any time since 1926.

"During the year 1935, the company was able to bring its preferred stock dividends up to date and to continue paying regularly each quarter the usual preferred dividend of 6 percent. At the same time, the common stock dividend was placed on a quarterly basis of ¼ of 1 percent, or 1 percent for the year." (Equal to $0.10 per share annually.)

Going into the World War II years, the Victor Adding Machine Co. was running in high gear. It claimed the right to a place among the leaders in the adding machine industry because Victor had pioneered many important improvements that later became universally accepted. The first Victors set a lead. They introduced strong, lightweight steel stampings to replace heavy castings.

Improved mass production methods and a host of technical innovations were introduced. In 1939, Victor set another lead by introducing a full-duty, compact adding machine to combine light weight with simplicity of mechanism.

Actually, two decades later, Victor history was repeating itself. In April, 1932, Oliver Johantgen, the original inventive genius behind the Victor product, died. In March, 1938, the appointment of Thomas O. Mehan as head of Victor's research and development was announced in these words:

"Mr. Mehan created and built the original Brennan adding machine, the name of which was later changed and sold to one of the larger adding machine manufacturers. . . As an inventive genius, he is second to none. . . His recent work in the development of small machines and the facilities now at his disposal point toward a creative career only begun." Mehan's original company, like Johantgen's, had failed, but Mehan had emerged from court proceedings with a clear right to his inventions despite the Remington purchase. Now he had joined forces with Victor and Victor once again was able to beat the industry with a small and inexpensive machine aimed at a mass market. Out of Mehan's lab and off the production line came the Victor 600 to be followed quickly by the Victor 700.

The 600 series started with a five-column keyboard machine capable of six column totaling. It weighed all of 8½ pounds and measured a slim 10¾ inches by 6¾ by 5¼ high. It sold for only $47.50. The two other machines in the series weighed slightly more, had additional features and larger capacities—seven and nine digit totaling. The prices were $55 and $70.

The 700 series paralleled the 600—three models, the same totaling capacities and prices—but introduced the 10-key keyboard. (The 10-key machine has a single key for each basic number, 0-1-2-3-4-5-6-7-8-9. To put or index 111.11 into the machine, the operator pushes the 1 key five times. The full keyboard machine, like the one in the top of the 600 series, has rows of basic numbers. To index 111.11, the operator simply goes across the row.) The weight of the 10-key machine was even less than that of the 600 series. Both series had far fewer parts than standard machines, and the 700 had only about two-thirds as many parts as the standards so that the manufacturing economies were major. The 10-key machine may seem less formidable to the untutored clerk or small businessman, but marketing experts say the difference between the 10-key and full-keyboard machine is largely one of individual preference. However, the series 700 did give Victor a significant sales advantage; the company could satisfy those individual preferences with machines that were otherwise comparable. And Vic-

In the late 30s Victor beat the industry
again with its small, inexpensive 600 series
(full keyboard) and 700 series (10-key
keyboard) adding machines utilizing the
same basic mechanism. Victor's 1939 sales
slogan was: "Sell the machine. Let the
customer have the keyboard of his choice."

tor was the only company to successfully manufacture both types simultaneously. As a 1939 Victor brochure said: "Sell the machine, let the customer have the keyboard of his choice."

By the time World War II military requirements had forced adding machine production down to only a necessary trickle, Victor brought out a full line of portables, adders, adder-subtractors, hand-operated and electric. The chassis and the basic mechanism designed by Mehan were to form the heart of postwar Victor machines from simple adders to sophisticated calculators.

Like the early Victor models, the 600 and 700 series of portables gained immediate and tremendous acceptances. During the three years from 1938 through 1941, Victor sales soared a phenomenal 301 percent.

With the renewed growth, Victor did not forget its employees. In 1938 the board of directors approved an amazing and singular step. Key management people, except for the Buehlers, were given a sizable bonus in stock and cash. And all employees on both the office and the factory payrolls were also given a bonus, based on seniority. Those who had been with Victor more than six months but less than five years were given a cash bonus equal to one percent of their 1937 gross pay. Those in the five- to ten-year bracket were given two percent of the 1937 pay, and those with over ten years' time were given three percent. At the same time, the board voted officially to continue the practice of giving all employees a Christmas basket made up of a turkey, a dozen oranges, five pounds of hard candy, a fruit cake, nuts and, surprisingly, a bottle of wine. Today the bottle of wine is gone, but employees still get a traditional Christmas turkey.

In preparation for a year or more, the Employees Security Fund was planned for announcement, and was announced, at the annual employees' banquet held in the Crystal Ballroom of the Edgewater Beach Hotel on the night following Pearl Harbor. It was one

Introduction of the Victor all-employee profit-sharing plan was announced to a somber Victor "family" at a dinner in the Edgewater Beach Hotel December 8, 1941, the day after the Japanese attack on Pearl Harbor. It was one of the first modern plans of its kind in Chicago industry.

of the first modern, all-employee profit-sharing plans in Chicago industry.

As mobilization for war proceeded in 1942, so too Victor shifted from peacetime to war production. Figuring machines were needed not only by defense plants but also by the armed services. But as matters worked out, the War Production Board named one small adding machine company to provide essential machines, while allowing Victor and other companies to maintain small production units and urgently needed repair services. (One specially designed and packaged Victor machine, the "Air Force Special," which computed in hours and minutes for figuring flight times, was even air dropped with invasion forces.) Very shortly after the declaration of war, Washington began tapping Victor's expertise in precision mass production. As a subcontractor, Victor was called upon to produce an aircraft directional compass, connectors for oxygen equipment, an optical gunsight used to aim turret guns on the B-24 bomber, and most complicated, an automatic fire control and cut-off unit for the upper machine gun turret in heavy bombers. A series of intricate gears prevented the gunner from swinging the power turret through an arc that would have allowed him to blast the bomber's tail or wing accidentally. On these contracts, Victor was working with Bendix, Emerson Electric and others. Then came the big one. In 1942 A.C. made a number of secret trips to Wright Field in Dayton, Ohio. The U. S. Army Air Force was looking for a company with the technical know-how and the scope to produce large quantities of a very exacting instrument under the most urgent priorities and tightest security conditions. It was the Norden bombsight, very possibly this country's second most secret weapon of World War II next to the atomic bomb. There were those in the top command at Victor who hesitated at the dimensions of the job. But to A.C. the Norden bombsight was a figuring machine. Victor was an expert at building figuring machines, and the country needed this one. The bombardier fed the machine essential information, the unit took control of the airplane during the final bomb run and gave the bombardier the on-target sighting for "bombs away."

From the minutes of the Victor board of directors meeting held April 3, 1942:

"Wherefore upon motion duly made, seconded and unanimously carried, the following resolution was adopted: Resolved that the directors approve the entry by this corporation into a contract with the War Department of the United States of America covering the manufacture by this company of 1,000 Mark XV, Model 7, bombsight assemblies and spare parts therefore on the basis of estimated cost plus six percent."

Carl L. Norden had perfected his bombsight over a period of years under contract to the U. S. Navy. When Victor became the prime contractor for the Air Force, it found that it was plunging into the demanding project almost on its own. The company received two sets of blueprints from the Air Force and, under guard, two complete bombsights. The Victor engineers were understandably proud of their abilities in precision manufacture but the thousands of gears, levers, bearings and shafts that made up the Norden sight demanded tolerances—millionths of an inch—unheard of in civilian manufacturing. Yet the blueprints received by Victor specified no dimensions for the mass production of parts or the assemblies. So the company set up a space in the back end of its building under security and put Tom Mehan in charge of some model makers and tool makers. They took one of the sights apart and measured each part and marked up the dimensions on the blueprints. They took only one of the sights apart because they needed the other one as a guide for reassembling the first one. After the job was done, Victor lined up subcontractors and sent a team out to the air depot in Sacramento, California, where there

Victor was the prime contractor for the Norden
bombsight used by the U.S. Army Air Force in
World War II. Bombsight No. 4120, used when the
Enola Gay dropped the first atomic bomb on
Hiroshima, was presented to the Smithsonian
Institution February 10, 1947. Present, from left,
were Rear Admiral W. S. Parsons, General Carl
Spaatz, A. C. Buehler, and Dr. Alexander Wetmore,
director of the Smithsonian.

was a service department for the Norden sight. The team learned something more about how to put it together and that was practically the only help Victor received. Carl Buehler III, A.C.'s oldest son, was a member of the team in Sacramento. After assisting in the training of bombsight technicians, he put on a uniform, joined the Office of Strategic Services and spent the next two years in Europe.

Despite these incredibly difficult circumstances, Victor was in full production within less than one year in a brand new plant that was engineered to be dust free and temperature controlled. More than 80 different companies, from the Able Tool Co. to the Wollensak Optical Co., were working under Victor direction on subcontracts. Victor's own employment jumped from 350 to more than 1,400. Manufacturing space at 3900 North Rockwell was expanded fourfold during the war, adding machine production was moved to rented space elsewhere, and a research unit under R. O. Buehler was established in Evanston where Tom Mehan, working with Northwestern University researchers, succeeded in adding a high altitude capability to the Norden sight. Victor was given the Army-Navy "E" award for production efficiency and Victor bombsight No. 4120, the sight that guided the Enola Gay on the run over Hiroshima on August 6, 1945, was donated to and is now on display in the Smithsonian Institution in Washington.

As World War II ended, Victor was ready with plans for expansion and for meeting the pent-up demand for figuring machines. And, with the lifting of wartime security, it was able with justifiable pride to advertise:

"Victor has both given and gained in its wartime assignment. Building the complete Norden bombsight called for the finest craftsmen, the latest in ultra-precision tools, the most modern of plant facilities and the highest possible engineering standards. The Norden bombsight . . . like an adding machine, must get the right answer from a flock of figures. It must determine accurately and quickly at just what point in space the bomb is to be released to hit the target. We at Victor, therefore, have assembled a group of unsurpassed craftsmen. We equipped them with the finest tools and facilities obtainable. These were added to the primary advantage of capitalizing on a peacetime experience of over a quarter of a century in the design and production of the finest figuring machines. These same craftsmen and facilities will soon turn again to building figuring machines for a world at peace."

Reconversion was less of a problem for Victor than for some other companies, particularly in that the company had just introduced a series of advanced models as the war began. But there were problems.

CHAPTER 7

The Right Combination

Once years before, H. L. Buehler had proposed to the Victor board of directors that the family's Buehler Bros. meat company be merged into Victor, then 88 percent owned by the family. H.L.'s plan was not adopted, but it points up what was a continuing problem for the Buehlers.

Here were four brothers, each with varying interests and varying viewpoints, charged with the responsibility of running two separate and widely disparate businesses. Through the years after the death of Carl Buehler, the four brothers formed the majority on the Victor board of directors. Sometimes they were together, sometimes they were split, sometimes ambitious officers of the company sought to divide the four in hopes of gaining a personal advantage. Then, too, there were times, in the eternal manner of all families, when someone would say, in effect, "Okay, if that's the way you feel, you do it." The brothers had various titles in the two companies, which titles were switched around to keep equality in the family. But the basic fact was simply the difficulties implicit in family management of two unrelated companies. Both were going concerns; both faced the obvious uncertainties of the period of postwar adjustment, a period that many business and government leaders saw as one of great opportunity while others, looking back to the Great Depression and to the recessions after World War I, viewed as one of certain economic trouble.

The solution to the family problem was apparent and in late 1945 the four brothers faced up to it: Divide the management and ownership of the businesses.

The big job was one of creating four equal packages. Each of the brothers had stock in Victor and in Buehler Bros. But it wasn't as simple as exchanging stock. Victor was the more valuable property so after two of the brothers (H.L. and R.O.) decided to take the meat business and the younger brother (C.C.) decided to join with A.C., there was the problem of raising the cash to make the scales balance on the meat side. To complicate matters, C.C. later decided that he'd go his own way and take straight cash for his holdings. A.C., plagued at the time with a late case of measles, arranged a variety of loans—a major one through the Continental Illinois National Bank and Trust Company of Chicago, and others from two old business associates, F. E. Henry, Jr. of McCaskey Register, and J. W. Schippmann of Haber Screw Machine Co., a long-time Victor supplier. In April 1946, C. C. Buehler resigned from the board of directors and A.C., except for his new indebtedness and a small percentage of the stock owned by employees, former employees and close friends, was sole owner of Victor. In the 1945 reconversion year, the company had earned just $148,000.

By this time, A.C.'s two sons were coming out of the armed services and both joined Victor for the same kind of training that A.C. had received when he was first watching the shop for his father. The elder son, Carl, had actually begun his Victor training as early as 1937 when he went to work during summer vacation on a grinding machine in the shop—"on the night shift where I wouldn't attract so much attention." Carl had been through the paces from factory floor to executive office and was executive vice president of the firm when he decided in 1963 to resign and devote full time to his young family.

Carl's younger brother, A.C., Jr., called Bert, born in 1923, was just getting well under way on his Victor training between college sessions when he went into the Navy for World War II service as an officer aboard a submarine escort patrol craft. Returning to Victor after the war, Bert served his apprenticeship, too, moving around the company from one department to another. Among other things, he visited every one of the company's distribution and sales offices in the United States and Canada. Eventually Bert Buehler became secretary of the corporation (1949) as his father had before him.

There was one particularly significant period during Bert's years of learning the business. He tells about it in these words:

"Alvin Bakewell has had a tremendous influence on the growth of the company. Bake asked for me at the time I was working in accounting and told me something very frankly. He said to me, 'I would like to try and teach you as much as I can about what I know about sales. Your dad gave me chances that nobody else would have ever given me, and I think I made it work for him and

I am forever grateful for the opportunities your dad has given me and what I was, therefore, able to provide for my family. And just as a little repayment I would like to take a son of his and teach him what I can about business machines and sales.' That was when I went to work for Bake. This was probably a smart thing all the way around and I think maybe he knew it was. If I didn't end up working for Bake, I really couldn't work for anybody directly other than my dad. I think Bake knew that this was probably the smartest thing to do—to have me work directly for somebody other than my dad for a while.

"Bake was not the easiest taskmaster in the world, but he is certainly one of the more admirable taskmasters. He expects a hell of a job done. Although he hasn't been sales manager for a number of years now, the basics that he and Dad laid down are still there."

Born in Brooklyn in 1901, Alvin F. Bakewell was fascinated as far back as he can remember with the sea and the ships that arrived from all over the world. At grade school age, he haunted the dock areas of lower Brooklyn, reading the names of the ships from far-off ports, touring the ships when he could get aboard, watching by the hour as the products of strange lands were unloaded. By high school age, he was uncommonly certain about his life's career; he'd go into the export business and, perhaps, see something of the world. Although later on he did attend Penn State briefly, Bakewell entered a commercial high school in furtherance of his aim and took typing, stenography, bookkeeping—and Spanish. The family was without means and Bakewell had worked at odd jobs throughout his school days. When finances made it impossible for him to continue at Penn State, Bakewell came home and got a job with a small import-export firm.

It was owned and operated by a group of Spaniards, and its main business was exporting American-made goods to Latin America. As the firm's only American-born employee, Bakewell prospered

"Super quiet" custom adding machines were examined by A. C. Buehler, then president; and A. F. Bakewell, then vice president and sales manager, in this 1951 photo.

and learned—not only the export business, but also, like thousands of Americans on a first tour of Spain, the difference between classical Castilian Spanish as taught in American schools and Latin American Spanish.

He was 26 years old, a bachelor, enjoying a modest success in his career as well as life in New York when Victor Adding Machine, by incredible chance, intervened. Bakewell tells about it:

"All of a sudden, out of the blue, I got a call from a man by the name of Hansard, Evan Hansard. He said he was the export manager for Victor Adding Machine and he had heard my name indirectly when he was traveling around South America. Would I like to go to work for Victor? I said, who the hell is Victor? And he said it was started in 1918 and made adding machines and was bringing out a portable typewriter and was building up its export business. He was kind of an abrupt man and he said he was leaving for Europe. If I wanted to find out more about Victor I could go into the New York office and talk to the people there but he wanted me to go out to Chicago and head up the export office from out there.

"This call did intrigue me so I went into Manhattan and visited the offices. The offices in those days were terrible. But there were some good people there and they thought well of the line. I was secretary and treasurer of the export firm by then and I wasn't at all dissatisfied, but I picked up the telephone and called them in Chicago and said, okay, I'd come. They wanted me in a week. I'll never forget my first day in Chicago. I'd never been to Chicago but I'd heard a lot about it and nothing much good. And it was raining like hell when I got off the train so you know what my first impression was.

"But that was more than 40 years ago and I've never once regretted my impulse. Not after I got out to the plant and met the people, particularly A.C.'s father, to me the most remarkable man in the world. He used to come in and sit in my office and talk to me about the company and about all sorts of different things. I'll put it this way, as I have told A.C. many times, I wouldn't work for anyone else. From the earliest days, it has been almost like being a member of the Buehler family.

"And you find the same spirit with most people here, not only for the Buehler family but for Victor itself. We love every dog-gone brick in this place. We all take the same interest in the progress the company has made. Sure, we have problems. But the thing is that when we have problems we all sit down and discuss them and try to solve them.

"There are a lot of successful companies and a lot of ways of running a successful company. I don't say we are unique or that we have the only answers. I do say we have some idea of the right way to do it and we try to do it that way. And I also say it wasn't done and isn't being done just accidentally. You can't be that lucky this very long length of time. When I first came here back in the 1920s, I felt immediately that Victor was a good place to work. I think we still have the same general spirit of people working together toward the same ends.

"We really didn't have much export business in those early days. There were all those problems you'd have with a figuring machine in relation to the drachma, the krona, the pound and the franc. So Victor was hoping for big things from the portable typewriter. But the typewriter didn't get off the ground.

"Just prior to the war, we brought out our portable adding machines and about the time we were going pretty well with it in the domestic market we had to stop because of the war. After the war, we knew we had an acceptable machine in the portables and there was a big demand for equipment so we had the right combination. What we had to do was to build up our sales organization.

"In this industry, perhaps in any industry, in addition to good products and research, you've got to have three things: you've got to have a good factory, and you've got to have a good sales organization with a good service department. I've been in sales but perhaps the factory is the most important in the combination. At least in this particular business, distribution costs are very high. So you'd better have a good efficient factory.

"The office equipment industry is very strong in Europe—and to some extent in Japan too. You see, office equipment is basic to a modern economy and after World War II under the Marshall Plan they provided money to build up the office equipment industry to help get Europe on its feet. Consequently, Europe came out of it with very modern factories in this industry. That's the story with typewriters. In the late 1950s, the Europeans with their up-to-date factories and low labor rates started to ship typewriters over here and the American companies, in typewriters and in other office machines, shifted their production overseas to take advantage of the wage rates. But we can still beat the manufacturer abroad today. With our factory, and our volume production, we even export to Japan.

"One day after the war A.C. came around to me and said, you've done a good job on export and I don't see why you can't do just as good a job on domestic sales, so why don't you take over. So I said, okay. It was just as simple as that. This was just about the time of the little reorganization we had in 1945 and 1946. We really started to push then."

After 1946, with A.C. in firm control and building his own organization, Victor headed into a period of remarkable growth that would not only make the company number one in the adding machine industry, but also generate diversification.

CHAPTER 8

Adding Machines + Cash Registers + Calculators

As soon as the proper papers could be drawn after World War II, Victor paid the Defense Plant Corp. the full and original price for the government-financed Norden plant at 3900 North Rockwell. Very promptly, production lines for adding machines were being rearranged to squeeze out even more manufacturing space.

In 1946 Victor sales hit an all-time high of $5,180,000. But that was only the start of the postwar boom. Sales reached $8,755,000 in 1947. This was enough to give Victor claim to title as "the world's largest exclusive manufacturer of adding machines."

75429

Even though production was sometimes strained to keep up with sales, management was doing far more than counting the dollars as they rolled in. Machines with greater capacity (totals up to one cent less than $1,000,000,000.00), flexibility, speed and performance were developed. The timing was right; even as the first of these postwar improvements reached the market in 1948 it was becoming evident that the cream had been skimmed off demand for smaller capacity machines. Sales that year climbed to a temporary high of $11,931,000, then sagged to $8,406,000 in 1949, and clicked ahead again in 1950. Despite the sales slowdown, an optimistic A. C. Buehler announced plans for a two-year plant expansion program that would double production facilities. And employed Oscar J. Sundstrand, the third of Victor's great inventors.

A remarkable man in the American tradition of practical inventors, Sundstrand was born in Rockford, Illinois on November 21, 1889, of immigrant Swedish parents. At age 18, with his brother G. David, he started to work on his first adding machine design. Seven years later, in 1914, the machine was successfully marketed by the Sundstrand Machine Tool Corp. of Rockford, an enterprise directed by two older brothers and Oscar and David. The adding machine was sold in 1927 to the Underwood-Elliott-Fisher Co. and Oscar became Underwood's inventor-in-residence until he decided on early retirement in 1949. The following year, A.C. persuaded him to lend his talents to Victor. With Victor support, Sundstrand would tinker, design and take on special projects, working in laboratories at his long-time home town, Hartford, Connecticut.

Sundstrand tackled his most important work for Victor. He took the basic design of the Mehan portable subtractor and made it into a modern, compact calculator. Subtractor is the term used for an adding machine that also offers the reverse capability of subtraction. Rather obviously, a subtractor can be used for multiplication and division. The process is not particularly laborious when the machine is equipped with a repeat key, as most modern machines are: 3 times 4 is 4 repeated 3 times and totaled. The calculator does the repeat addition (or subtraction) internally when it is asked to multiply or divide and thus offers the user a machine that will efficiently and automatically perform all four mathematical functions.

In the earliest history of figuring machines, devices that would add, subtract, multiply and divide were built. But it wasn't until Dorr E. Felt produced his Comptometer in the 1880s that business had a practical calculator and one that did not put a self-defeating burden of mental gymnastics on the operator. (The operator had to learn a system to calculate with the Comptometer, but it was easily taught and learned.) The Marchant company, now part of SCM, Inc., and the Monroe company, now part of Litton Industries, successfully marketed fully mechanical calculators after 1920 and the Friden company was successful with another version in 1934. But these machines did not print out; the answers were shown on dial faces. It was not until just prior to World War II that Remington produced a listing or printing calculator. However, the Remington was complicated to operate and so was the Underwood printing calculator.

When Sundstrand went to work for Victor, A.C. told him what he wanted: a Victor. That is, a compact, simple machine, easy to operate, dependable and fast. It was no easy task, even for the experienced Sundstrand.

The first working model came out of Sundstrand's shop in 1952. After refinements were made, eight machines were built and placed for test purposes in Victor's own accounting department in October, 1953. Still further modifications followed, particularly to fit the machine to Victor's mass production technique and also to simplify the operator's task. Even so, Sundstrand and Victor's management were still dissatisfied with the method of division. Division being the least used in business of the four mathematical functions, it was decided to go ahead with an adder-subtractor-multiplier and Victor's first automatic printing calculator went into full production in May of 1954. The improved version with simplified division went into production 18 months later (November, 1955).

Meanwhile, Victor was showing steady and sometimes spectacular progress. The regular product line had been broadened and improved. In May, 1952, the one millionth Victor machine had rolled off the production line—and had been subjected to a "breakdown" test. Automatic machinery operated the unit continuously eight hours a day, six days a week. After 16,440,705 machine operations (cycles) and 36 weeks, the machine finally stopped; a minor electrical switch, not a mechanical part, had failed. In that same year, the company had a direct factory sales and service force of more than 500 working out of 39 domestic branches, more than double the pre-war number of branches. It was also selling through 600 exclusive dealers and several thousand non-exclusive dealers in this country and it had a strong overseas selling system of 62 distributors. With 20 to 25 percent of the total U.S. adding machine market, it was strengthening its position in the industry and sales were booming up to the $15 million mark.

And, A.C. was planning the first in a series of successful mergers.

For some years A.C. had been thinking—and worrying—about Victor's good, long-time customer, the McCaskey Register Co. Thinking back over the McCaskey relationship, A.C. comments: "Originally, the McCaskey register was just an adding machine on a cash drawer. It was inexpensive and they did a fantastic job with it. At one time, McCaskey accounted for about 25 percent of our volume. Then, as our volume grew, the percentage got to be less and less; 15, 12, and 10 percent. We did start supplying McCaskey

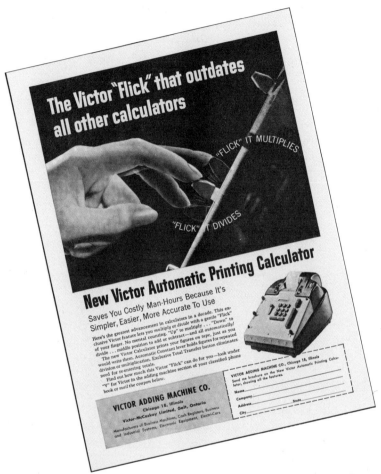

The first Victor automatic printing calculator went into full production in May of 1954. This adder-subtractor-multiplier was followed a year later by another machine (above) that also included division. Introduced in June, 1968, the Series 10 grand total printing calculator (right) is one of the fastest electro-mechanical calculators available today.

with our duplex adding machine when it came along. The merchant would keep his cash sales in one total and add up his credit sales in the other, so that at the end of the day he'd have a total of the credit extended as well as the cash received. But the cash register people were bringing out more sophisticated registers all the time and well, to tell the truth, the McCaskey management was getting along in years and their people weren't too interested in spending any money on anything new. They were kind of happy to let the business go along the way it was; after all, basically their business was selling sales books. So one day I went to the president, Hi Henry, and said, 'Listen, it is very seldom that our people bump into your people. Most of your sales are rural and we're playing the cities. Now I know you have an exclusive contract and I'm not trying to break that. But why don't you let us sell cash registers out of our branches. We'd change the design and we'd pay you a royalty on every machine we sell.' Well, he didn't know about that; our sales organization was stronger than his and he was afraid we'd interfere with his business. I kept coming back to him and pressing him just a little bit. Finally one day he said, 'Why don't you just buy us out?' So we did that, for cash and preferred stock. We didn't want to be in the printing business; we wanted the cash register end. So I went to National Carbon Coated Paper Co., which was doing a similar business, and sold them the printing.

"This was our first acquisition, if you want to call it that. But I wasn't thinking in terms of an acquisition at all. It was a means of protecting our sales and, hopefully, of increasing them by building up the cash register sales. Eventually, we sold the McCaskey plant in Alliance, Ohio, and moved all the production up here to Chicago. And we finally parted with the credit register side, too. Better business systems for handling paperwork were being developed so we got out of it. But we like being in the cash register business and we intend to go right along developing registers and sales."

The McCaskey merger not only gave Victor a foothold in a vast new allied field, but it also contributed immediately to Victor's sales. With Victor's own gains, combined sales hit $23,092,000 in 1953.

Another Victor move about the same time did not turn out so well. In fact, it started off unpleasantly and ended that same way. In 1949 on a trip to Hawaii, A.C. came down with an illness that turned into pneumonia. After he was up and about, A.C. was ordered by his doctors, nervous about his early history of lung ailments, to take a long convalescence in the dry sunshine of Arizona. An ardent golfer, A.C. was soon out on the golf course again —with the aid of an electric golf cart. As a user, he was annoyed at the cheap construction and the poor or inconvenient design. As a manufacturer of quality products, he was sure his plant could turn out a much superior cart. As a businessman, he could see the possibilities in a major new product aimed at an ever-increasing leisure-time market. In 1953 Victor began manufacturing the Electri-Car, a superior cart for golf courses, also offered eventually in a variety of models to industrial customers as a personnel carrier, a truck, an emergency fire wagon, a mobile maintenance shop. Inside of six years, Victor was a major factor in the industry, and wished it weren't.

Even though A.C. had it figured right. The market was there, but so was everybody else. Particularly, there were too many back-alley garage mechanics in the business, assembling carts out of new or used parts, selling a few, dumping the rest at fire sale prices. Everybody was selling price while Victor was working away at improving the product. (Just one example: the front hood was raised higher to prevent embarrassment to lady golfers.) Not that A.C. hadn't anticipated cutthroat competition. "I thought this would be something you could sell," he once said, "and that part was right. Almost every course has them today. Then I figured it would be like the automobile business in the early days. One year there were 126 different manufacturers represented in the New York auto show, but look what you have now. I thought that somewhere along the line the golf cart business would simmer down, too, to a few good-size outfits that could handle the distribution. I still think it will work that way, but it was just taking too long."

A.C. made the hard decision, possibly the hardest decision a manager has to make: to back down on a favored project, to take your lumps now even though the chance remains good that another year, another two years, of red ink will prove the project. In 1960 Victor assumed a $575,000 debt run up by its principal Electri-Car distribution subsidiary, reduced manufacture and two years later put the operation on a service and repair basis.

It was a minor detour, all in all. Elsewhere, the evidence of progress was easy to see. It had taken Victor 34 years—from 1918 until 1952—to produce 1,000,000 figuring machines. Just six years later, in 1958 as the company was celebrating its 40th anniversary, machine number 1,500,000 came off the line. In 1952 Victor completed a $2,000,000 addition to the main plant, increasing manufacturing space by more than 130,000 square feet. And manufacturing efficiency, that essential ingredient of Victor's success, was not being neglected: in 1959, for instance, $1,250,000 was invested in machinery, equipment and new tools for the new Victor models and followed with a $2,000,000 expenditure in 1960. At the same time, the dividend on the common stock was still being held to 15 cents a share on the 1,000,000 shares then outstanding.

Internal growth, simply doing the job better, putting out more and better products: these were still A.C.'s main concerns. But he often considered acquisitions and new fields. Particularly he was concerned in the 1950s—and later on—with that new phenomenon of the office machine world, electronic data processing, the computer. Repeatedly, he discussed it with the board of directors and with outside consultants. Should Victor take the plunge? Should Victor, a leader in mechanical figuring machines, try to become a manufacturer of computers and data processing hardware? A.C. took a cold-blooded look at the technology involved, the fantastic developmental costs and the equally impressive loss figures being reported by many companies in the field. He voted no. In 1957 A.C. talked about "that desk-top wonder," the automatic printing calculator, and its ability to provide the everyday right answers for business. "Mammoth electronic computers fill a real need for the giants of industry," he said, "but the mass market for office automation will remain in the domain of the old-line manufacturers who have met the figuring machine needs of American business, both large and small, since the pioneer days of the still indispensable adding machine."

Realistically, a course was rejected that was to bring a number of companies with larger resources than Victor to near-bankruptcy and forced merger. At the same time, it was seen that there always would be a basic need for figuring machines, that indeed there would be an even greater call for machines to supply the raw material needed to satisfy the vast appetites of computers, small, medium, and large.

Even so, despite these very correct business judgments, A.C. kept an open mind—conditions might change, unexpected opportunity might arise, a way for Victor to enter the computer field profitably could develop. At the same time, A.C. launched a search for the electronic technology that would extend the top line of Victor calculators, giving them computer-age capability and speed.

And, as important as anything else, A.C. set about finding the best means of assuring the corporate growth of Victor.

CHAPTER 9

Ingredients for a Merger

Typically, the modern American corporation of any size and maturity is in the hands of professional managers. The founding genius, the individual entrepreneur who built the company, has long since passed into history. In fact, a search of the stockholder records may not turn up the family name at all and only business scholars know that the modern and meaningless name of the corporation, JJ Inc., was once Jones & Jones. In marked contrast, when the Victor Adding Machine Co. celebrated its 40th anniversary in 1958, the company had been dominated from its earliest

days by one family and for most of those years by its chief executive officer, A. C. Buehler, the company's oldest employee in point
of service. Perhaps even more rare among large industrial corporations, Victor was still privately owned. A.C. and his family owned
all but a small fraction of the stock and that small fraction was
tightly held by friends, key employees and business associates.
Noteworthy, too, is the fact that Victor was a growth company;
money that could have gone into family pockets by way of dividends went instead into building growth.

But the time was coming, A.C. realized, when Victor's private
status could hamper growth and create other problems. Without
a publicly traded (and priced) stock to offer to other companies,
Victor's easiest avenue to corporate mergers was blocked. And, if
the need should ever arise for large amounts of capital, Victor
could not easily turn to the equity markets to sell new common
or preferred stock or bonds or debentures. Then, on the personal
level, there was the spectre of inheritance tax problems that could
force the family into a ruinous disposal to meet the federal tax bill.

The obvious solution was to "go public," for A.C. to put a certain percentage of his own stock in the hands of an investment
banking firm, and have the shares sold to the public. Over a period
of years, A.C. discussed this solution with a number of investment
banking houses but there was never a meeting of minds. A.C. and
the financial men, unfamiliar with Victor and overly impressed
with the diversified giants that formed Victor's main competition,
differed sharply on the current and future value of the company.

Remembering the times and the problems, A.C. says: "In the
first place, we had so much stock in the family—at least, I did; and
there came a time when I couldn't give it away anymore. I'd been
passing it along to the family, but you reach a point where making
gifts is less attractive because of gift taxes. So there isn't any sense
in giving any more away.

"So what would happen if I had stepped out of the picture when we were still privately owned? You don't hear about it too much, but it happens to a lot of private companies. The family has got to sell out to pay the taxes. Well, everybody knows it and nobody offers full value. Sure, the family can perhaps hold out a couple of years by paying Internal Revenue six percent interest on the taxes as finally determined. You can even go public during that time but that, too, is likely to be a rush job. You don't want to sell anything under those conditions. The best way to establish value is to have willing sellers and willing buyers. No matter what Internal Revenue thinks then, the market establishes the worth. I felt I had to do something of this kind to establish the value of Victor. Another thing that can happen when you don't have a public market value is that when it comes to establishing the taxable value, Uncle Sam may capitalize your goodwill. And that can be murder. He'll take your net worth and maybe double it and say that that's how you make your money, on your goodwill or reputation. But if you have to sell the business, you'll be lucky to get much more than the net worth for it. The only way to fight back is to find comparable businesses where there is an established market price. Otherwise, you'll find yourself paying tax on Uncle Sam's figure with the goodwill factor thrown in. So I wanted to clear all this up, but at the time I was talking to the investment banking people, the underwriters, the best offer I could get was $18 a share. That is, the net proceeds from a sale of Victor stock would be $18 a share and the initial market price for the remaining shares would be around $18.

"Now we had 1,000,000 shares of stock at the time, so the best offer was worth $18,000,000 for the whole company. I told them I'd think about it and I just kept right on thinking about it."

A peculiar combination of circumstances involving some of these same tax and ownership problems eventually provided a solution. At first glance it wasn't the best of all possible solutions, but A.C. made it work. The solution came in the form of the Comptometer Corporation, pioneer in the figuring machine business and a Chicago neighbor of Victor's. A LaSalle Street investment banker had first suggested a Comptometer-Victor merger to A.C. right after the end of World War II. At the time, Comptometer was also privately owned and the merger conversations came to naught when it appeared that several large Comptometer owners would not agree to the sale of the family company no matter how beneficial the circumstances. Originally founded as the Felt & Tarrant Manufacturing Company, Comptometer had had a total of 11 stockholders, members of the two founding families and a couple of key employees, when Dorothea Felt Noyes and her husband perished in the unbelievable Coconut Grove nightclub fire of 1942 in Boston. Her stock had been placed in trust in a Chicago bank where the administrators were uneasy at keeping the bulk of an estate tied up in a private stock, worth only book value at best. Then in 1945, Robert Tarrant, son of the co-founder, died and created for his family the very situation that was to worry A.C. later on. Quickly, the bank trustees and the Tarrant family agreed that a public offering of stock would solve the problem of both the bank and the family. There was little the other stockholders could do and stock was offered for sale in 1946. The following year, Felt & Tarrant, as it was known until 1957, was listed on the New York Stock Exchange. Thus, when two directors of Comptometer came to A.C. with a merger proposal 15 years after the first talks, A.C. was interested not only for straight business reasons, but also, and perhaps mainly, as a way to go public. A merger with Comptometer would in one single step make Victor a public company and give it a New York Stock Exchange listing.

Comptometer was the brainchild of Dorr Eugene Felt, a story book American inventor who succeeded where the best brains, from Blaise Pascal onward, had failed—in the creation of a practi-

Dorr Eugene Felt, inventor of the first commercially successful key-driven calculating machine—the Comptometer— is shown with the working mechanism of his invention. Above is early model in its wooden case.

cal, working calculating machine. Born March 18, 1862, on a farm in Rock County, Wisconsin, near Beloit, Felt had only a country school education through the first year of high school. Mechanically-minded, he was working in a Beloit machine shop at age 14. At some point between 14 and 20, when he moved to Chicago in pursuit of this great idea, Felt was inspired by watching the control mechanism of a wood planing machine. By setting a ratchet at one notch, the planer would strip off so much wood; at another notch, the planer would go deeper. Why not use the same system to make a calculating machine? Instead of lowering the plane an eighth of an inch or a quarter of an inch, the movement of the ratchet would indicate a number. The real problem would be in constructing the mechanism to make the first ratchet, or wheel, "carry" to the second. Years later, Dorr Felt set down his impressions of his early efforts (quoted in J. A. V. Turck's *Origin of Modern Calculating Machines*):

"Watching the planer-feed set me to scheming on ideas for a machine to simplify the hard grind of the bookkeeper in his day's calculation of accounts.

"I realized that for a machine to hold any value to an accountant, it must have greater capacity than the average expert accountant. Now I knew that many accountants could mentally add columns of four-digit figures at a time, so I decided that I must beat that in designing my machine. Therefore, I worked on the principle of duplicate denominational orders that could be stretched to any capacity within reason. The plan I finally settled on is displayed in what is generally known as the 'Macaroni Box' model. This crude model was made under rather adverse circumstances.

"The construction of such a complicated machine from metal, as I had schemed up, was not within my reach from a monetary standpoint, so I decided to put my ideas in wood.

"It was near Thanksgiving Day of 1884 and I decided to use the holiday in the construction of the wooden model. I went to the grocer's and selected a (wooden) box which seemed to me to be about the right size for the casing. It was a macaroni box, so I have always called it the 'macaroni box model.' For keys I procured some meat skewers from the butcher around the corner and some staples from a hardware store for the key guides and an assortment of elastic bands to be used for springs. When Thanksgiving Day came, I got up early and went to work with a few tools, principally a jackknife.

"I soon discovered that there were some parts which would require better tools than I had at hand for the purpose, and when night came, I found that the model I had expected to construct in a day was a long way from being complete or in working order. I finally had some of the parts made out of metal and finished the model soon after New Year's Day, 1885."

Experimenting further in wood, Felt improved his machine and finally in the fall of 1886 produced his first working model in metal. He was 24 years old, living in Chicago, and had, fortunately, found a man willing to sponsor him.

This was Robert Tarrant, the owner of a machine shop and forge located at the foot of Illinois Street near the Chicago River. Tarrant's main business was making and repairing iron work for ships in the Lakes trade. Intrigued with Felt's ideas, he signed Felt on as a helper at $6 a week and gave him a bench in the rear of the shop where Felt could work on his invention. Over a period of time, Tarrant advanced Felt about $5,000 for materials and parts and other expenses involved in the development of the calculating machine. In return for his $5,000, Tarrant got an equal interest in a partnership the two formed in 1887 and in Felt & Tarrant Manufacturing Company when it was incorporated two years later.

Over a lifetime, Felt held 46 U. S. patents and 25 patents in foreign countries. The most important of these was the basic

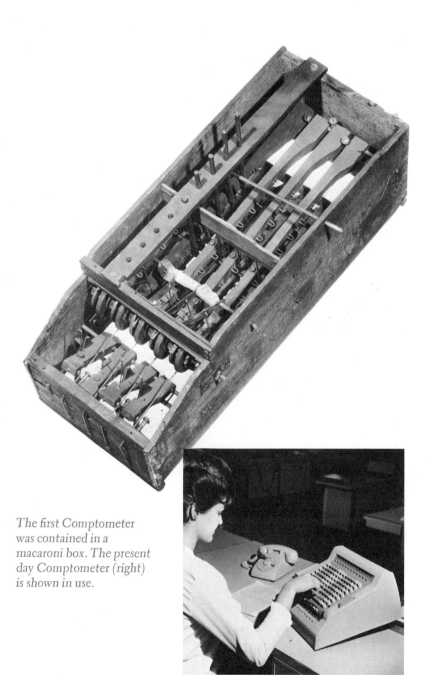

The first Comptometer
was contained in a
macaroni box. The present
day Comptometer (right)
is shown in use.

Comptometer patent issued July 19, 1887. The distinguishing feature of the Comptometer then, when it was being marketed as the first practical calculating machine, and the distinguishing feature through the years, was this: the Felt machine was key-driven, i.e., depressing and releasing the key actuated the adding (or subtracting or multiplying or dividing) mechanism and the result appeared simultaneously in the answer dials. Almost all modern adding and calculating machines are so-called key-set devices, e.g., the key merely indexes the number while a hand crank or an electric motor bar actuates the performing mechanism. In that it is a single-motion machine, the Comptometer is faster in the hands of a skilled operator than its two-motion competitors. But the modern two-motion machine performs the arithmetic functions internally while the Comptometer did and does place a larger mental burden on the operator. For instance, to subtract on the two-motion machine of today, the operator throws the subtract keys, indexes the figure as he would in writing them down, and hits the motor bar. On the Comptometer, a system of coordinates is used for subtraction. Felt's system was simple, but it does have to be learned. As Turck comments in his book on calculating machines:

"A superficial examination of one of the instruction books of the Comptometer will convince most anyone that it is not only the mechanism of the machine that made the modern calculator so valuable to the business world, but also the schemes laid down for its use. The instructions for figuring multiplication, subtraction, division, square root, cube root, interest, exchange, discount, English currency, etc., involved hard study to devise such simple methods and rules. The instruction books written by Felt for the 'Comptometer, the Modern Calculator,' reflect the genius disclosed in the invention of the machine itself."

Felt had succeeded in the task he set himself; his machine had almost unlimited capacity, in contrast to the adding machines that were to come along, provided only that the operator would apply himself and learn the easy rules.

By the summer of 1887, Felt had built a total of eight Comptometers. One he took to Washington where the U. S. Treasury was "favorably impressed" and agreed after a trial period to order "three or four machines for the use of this Office." Others were placed with Chicago companies and Felt immediately ran into a problem that was to turn into a profitable sideline in later years. The operators had to be trained; eventually the Comptometer training schools emerged as temporary office help agencies. But Felt's very first salesman completed his course, called on half a dozen companies and wrote Felt that he would have time to call upon no more. The Equitable Gas Light & Fuel Co., now Peoples Gas Light & Coke Co. of Chicago, had hired him and his Comptometer to work in the accounting department.

In any event, the Comptometer was a success. On June 11, 1889, Felt was issued a patent for his second machine, the Comptograph, which was a listing machine. The Comptometer was not and is not a recording or listing machine; answers showed on window dials to be read off and entered into journals and other business papers. But the competing Burroughs machines did have a print-out. The first Comptographs were not particularly successful in that, although they were key-driven, a second and cumbersome lever motion was necessary to actuate the printing unit. Later Felt switched to the key-set, two-motion system for his Comptograph and the machine had good sales, particularly in Europe.

The production of the Comptograph was fortunate in that it provided a solution to a difficult problem. Increasingly, the Felt & Tarrant partnership became an uneasy one. The older Tarrant was cautious while Felt, a combination dreamer and hardheaded businessman, was full steam ahead. Finally in 1902 they agreed to go their separate ways—almost. Tarrant would take the Compto-graph and Felt would take the Comptometer. Two companies were formed and set up in such a way that each man would have ultimate control of one company, but at the same time each would participate in the profits of both companies. It was agreed that Felt would have the controlling 51 percent of Felt & Tarrant Manufacturing Company, the company producing the Comp-tometer, while Tarrant would have the controlling interest in the Comptograph Company. This arrangement apparently worked well until World War I killed off the main source of Comptograph revenues, the sales in Europe. The Comptograph, its plant and assets, were reabsorbed by Felt & Tarrant Manufacturing Com-pany and the business liquidated. Although Felt & Tarrant was still getting calls for Comptograph parts as late as 1934, Felt was uninterested in trying to revive the machine after World War I. For one thing, the machine was cumbersome, very heavy and more expensive than Felt's beloved Comptometer and, thus, was in need of a drastic redesign. Too, the competition was concentrat-ing on the recording end of the business.

In the modern era, in the years after World War II, that same competition fell more and more heavily on the Comptometer, too. The machine was still highly favored by the national corporations with their high-volume accounting departments. But steadily the recording adders and calculators were narrowing the Comptome-ter's market. With Dorr Felt's death at age 68 in 1930, manage-ment of the company had eventually passed to Raymond J. Koch, the husband of Virginia Felt, one of Felt's four daughters. Koch had been educated as a civil engineer (Armour Institute of Tech-nology, now part of the Illinois Institute of Technology) and had worked his way up to administrative positions with an electrical manufacturing company when he was asked to join Felt & Tarrant a few years before Felt's death. Koch became treasurer of the com-pany and then president in 1934.

The original "macaroni box" Comptometer was
presented to the Smithsonian Institution in 1937.
Dr. Charles G. Abbot, Secretary of the Smithsonian,
accepts it from Mr. and Mrs. Raymond J. Koch.
Koch was president of Felt and Tarrant
Manufacturing Company at that time. Name was
changed to Comptometer Corporation in 1957.

Increasingly in the years after World War II, Koch was concerned about Comptometer's one-product position and its lagging sales. Research and development was his answer. Once he set out on an imaginative project only to be confounded by the times. He asked the renowned research division at his old alma mater to design an electronic calculator, one that would leapfrog the electromechanical calculators then being brought out and put Comptometer into the developing computer age. Armour complied and a quarter of a million dollars later displayed a working model with tremendous capacity and speed. But there was trouble. The Armour researchers had made use of the technology available—vacuum tubes—and the machine itself was wired into a bulky cabinet packed with tubes. The machine may have had possibilities, but things never got to a test; by the time Armour completed its work, the tiny, efficient transistor had been born and was being substituted where possible for vacuum tubes. Obviously, Armour would have to start all over and redesign the circuitry, substituting these new transistors.

But that would take time and Koch had trapped himself on this and other projects—acquisitions and new products—that might also take time to work out. In the 1940s, he had instituted a profit-sharing pension plan for all Comptometer employees and he had insisted upon compulsory retirement at age 65.

Now he was approaching that age and he felt that he must honor his own rule. Further, he felt that it would be unwise for him to launch Comptometer into radical new fields and then dump the responsibility for making a success on the shoulders of someone else. The responsibility would not only have fallen on someone else, but on someone unfamiliar with the background. Because Comptometer's management was pretty well of an age, the company was going to have to go outside for a new president.

Short of retirement age, Koch moved up to chairman (1956)

and asked the board to choose a president. Thus, began a turbulent period for Comptometer. Outsiders were brought into management and outsiders both were invited in and bought their way in as members of the board. Ideas for new products, for diversification and acquisitions, for reorganization, abounded. Some were good and some were terrible, but through the latter part of the 1950s, things were popping at Comptometer.

Meanwhile, a quiet resolution of a long-standing Comptometer problem permanently changed the face of the corporation. The problem grew out of Europe's economic troubles in the reconstruction period after World War II. Always Comptometer had enjoyed good acceptance in England, but after the war the company ran into progressively tougher restrictions designed to protect British industry. An early British restriction refused an import license for machines that were directly competitive with an English-made product. Under this regulation, Comptometer could ship its electrified machine to England, but could not sell its standard manual machine because a British company, Control Systems Limited, was making a similar key-driven calculator. The next regulation demanded British content in imported machines. Comptometer met that one by completing the machine in Chicago, taking it apart, shipping the parts to England and having the machine assembled once again by British labor—assemblers were recruited from Comptometer's extensive repair and service organization. Then the British tightened up again; machines had to have some British-made parts. As matters ended, Comptometer had a full-scale assembly plant going with all the parts being made by British subcontractors. There were some benefits: the British market was maintained, machines could be shipped from England to other Commonwealth countries where restrictions barred the U.S.-made machine, and to any dollar-short country on the European continent where pounds might be available for payment.

The British operation was profitable, and reached a point where it was accounting for 25 percent of Comptometer's total volume. But there was a catch. Taking that much volume out of the Chicago plant meant soaring unit costs in Chicago and profit margins perilously close to zero. One of the new managers, a man with a good record, but no experience in the figuring machine industry, thought he had an answer for that. After looking over the Chicago plant, he decided overhead costs could be cut and profit margins improved by firing most of the inspection force.

With anguish, Raymond Felt Koch, the chairman's son who had become company secretary, recalls the incident: "We had one quality control inspector for every eight production workers and that seemed very high to these people. But they just didn't know the business. It is like few others. You know, you think of a watch as a precision instrument. But no one knows or cares if the watch is 30 seconds fast or slow over a period of weeks. A watch is never 100 percent right. But a figuring machine has got to be 100 percent right, all the time. If it is wrong one time out of a thousand or out of ten thousand times, it is worthless, worse than worthless. So they got rid of the inspectors and all hell broke loose with the product. Then, just about that time, the British eased their restrictions. But instead of doing the logical thing, instead of bringing the English production back here, which would have solved the overhead problem, the operating people wanted to switch all our production to England. They didn't succeed at that, so they recommended the sale of our entire English operation, including our trademark and the right to the Comptometer name in England, to the Control Systems people. And they sold it at net book value. We didn't get a cent for our name or the goodwill which had been built up over a period of many years. We lost that entire market and then signed a contract with Control Systems to have all our machines manufactured in England and shipped back here.

In 1961, as soon as the inventory of parts was used up, all production in Chicago stopped."

The most exciting product brought into Comptometer during this period was the Electrowriter.

The history of the telecommunications device goes back to World War II. The Signal Corps was given the research assignment of developing a system that could be used by advance units to report back to the rear on enemy positions, terrain, fortifications and other factors that might be useful in troop tactics and in artillery and air strikes. Of course, there was the telephone. But the military wanted something that would provide a record, to reduce the possibility of garbled meanings, and also to give officers a graphic representation showing, for instance, the relationship of a hill to a forest. Something that would transmit a hand-drawn picture together with notations on such things as distances and numbers would be the ticket.

The war ended before the project got much beyond the "think" stage, but the idea and its possible civilian as well as military applications very much intrigued a Signal Corps colonel named Peter G. S. Mero. After the war, Mero became director of communications for the American Red Cross, where he worked closely with telephone companies on emergency communications systems for the Red Cross disaster service. At the same time, he put his own money into research on the graphic communication idea.

By 1949, Mero's efforts had resulted in a prototype and a basic patent. This, again, was the age of the vacuum tube and the prototype was so bulky that commercial people considered it unsalable. It took Mero, a dedicated man with a world of enthusiasm, until 1955 to see to the development of a transistorized model. Mero had been working closely with American Telephone and Telegraph (the Bell System labs had produced the first transistors) and there was the thought that AT&T's Teletype Corp. in Chicago might manufacture the device. But, by this time, the anti-trust division of the Justice Department was officially frowning on AT&T activities outside of voice communication.

At this point in history, Mero made contact with Comptometer, where some of the new management people had come out of a telephone equipment manufacturing background. In the spring of 1958 Comptometer bought a Mero-promoted company, Union Thermo-electric Corp., and at the same time acquired the rights to Mero's Electrowriter. A year later, Comptometer had pre-production models ready for testing and the first system was installed in October of 1959. But the Electrowriter was still a long way from making its mark. Still further and substantial development costs were to come, production had to be set up, and a sales force was needed.

Meanwhile, Comptometer was moving rapidly in other directions. It entered the sports field by acquiring first the Burke Golf Equipment Corporation, a top-rated maker of golf clubs, and then the Worthington Ball Company, a leading maker of golf balls. With the help of Lloyd Drexler, a Chicago consultant with a background in finance and acquisitions, Comptometer got into another field, the production of business forms, by acquiring the Nebraska Salesbook Company of Lincoln, Nebraska; the Tex-N-Set Manifold Co. of Arlington, Texas; and the National Systems and Forms Co. of Passaic, New Jersey.

To put all this together, Comptometer paid out its own and borrowed cash and issued new stock to exchange for the stock of its marriage partners. Naturally enough, more than a little expense was involved, sometimes unforeseen problems emerged and the development and promotional costs of the Electrowriter were a major and continuing drain.

Behind the closed doors of the meetings of the board of directors, tension and division mounted in 1961. Sales were increasing, but not dramatically. Comptometer volume in 1956 had amounted to $15,720,000. By the end of 1960, sales for the year amounted to $20,363,000. The earnings picture, however, was dismal. In the period from 1956 to 1959 the corporation sustained losses of $77,000, $253,000, $560,000, and $287,000, before reporting a profit of $516,000 in 1960. But the profit for 1960 and the red figures as shown for 1959 and 1958 were after a decision to defer the very heavy Electrowriter costs. The amount deferred in 1960 would have turned the $516,000 profit into a deficit of $823,000.

At the same time, the number of Comptometer shares outstanding had been increased from 671,000 to 850,000 (and would go to 981,000 in 1961), and there was more than $2,000,000 outstanding in convertible debentures and more than $3,000,000 in short-term bank debt.

Matters came to a head in early 1961 when the board of directors was asked to approve plans for a new convertible debenture financing of $5,000,000. "I stood up on my hind legs and said, 'over my dead body,'" the senior Koch recalls. Koch was joined by Peter Mero, then executive vice president, a director, and the holder of a sizable block of stock through a stock option and as a result of transactions involving Union Thermo and Electrowriter.

And it was Mero, dedicated as always to his Electrowriter, who had the better idea to provide Comptometer the funds and stability it needed. He, and later Koch, called upon A. C. Buehler and found him receptive.

CHAPTER 10

An Amazing Fit

Opposition within Comptometer's leadership to a merger with Victor collapsed when a determined Raymond J. Koch, backed up by Peter Mero, threatened a proxy fight; and when Lloyd Drexler, by then vice chairman of the board, chief executive officer and a director, agreed that the Victor merger should be explored.

Drexler, it turned out, was a key figure in hammering out the details of the merger with A.C., tentatively announced in July of

1961. His had been an active and interesting career. He earned undergraduate and graduate degrees at Northwestern University and served on the faculty, teaching economics and finance, before World War II. During the war he was a flying officer and was shot down over Germany, captured and escaped on five different occasions. After the war he was on the faculty at Roosevelt University part time, devoting his major energies to successfully building up a family-owned business, Northern Illinois Steel Co. At the same time, he entered banking and also acted as a consultant on mergers and corporate financing. Drexler got into the Comptometer picture when he set up a sale and leaseback arrangement on Comptometer's plants to provide capital for the company. (The money was provided by the Wesil Corp., formed by Drexler and his associates. As part of the deal, Wesil was given options on 125,000 shares of Comptometer stock. The options were later to prove highly profitable.) Still later, Drexler was instrumental in building Allied Products Corp. into a substantial corporation.

Thinking back to the spring of 1961, Drexler says:

"From the time we first met A. C. Buehler and got a good look into his techniques and methodology, we became increasingly sold on the eventual outcome. Comptometer was an old-line manufacturer of business equipment. The term itself, Comptometer, is virtually part of the language. They came into the field long before most other companies. They, however, did not do anything in the way of significant development in this whole area of office automation. As a result, the company had inevitably entered into a period of decline. A number of acquisitions, primarily in the leisure and office forms field, gave them the added income to keep the company alive. However, because of conflicting opinions within the company, very serious squabbles developed and it got pretty vicious, as these things often do.

Principals of Victor Adding Machine Co.
and Comptometer Corporation shake
hands to seal merger of Comptometer
into Victor in October, 1961. A. C.
Buehler of Victor is shown at left with
Raymond J. Koch of Comptometer.

"At the time, Victor evidenced an interest and it was very opportune for the shareholders of Comptometer. However, there were some very complex negotiations. You're dealing with values which are largely intangible when you're talking about combining any two enterprises. The tangible aspects are the significant, but at the same time the least significant. Any combination, to be successful, must offer synergism, the possibility of making two and two equal more than four. And in this area, it is the human aspect that's more important, not the product and not the basic data.

"So what did we find at Victor? We saw an organization that was far advanced and original and creative in its thinking with an advanced organizational and human relations philosophy.

"Just one example, on the human relations side—Victor was integrating Negroes back when labor was plentiful and there was no real pressure. The company didn't wait until public questions were raised about its employment practices. This is a company that follows what the psychologists would call the human relations model of organization, rather than the authoritarian model. This is the way Victor was long before 1961 when we first saw them, and still today most of the giants are following the theory of the authoritarian model even though there is clear cut statistical evidence that there is a significant difference in favor of the human relations model. Victor has been willing to think in terms of the individual and it, therefore, is able to utilize the resources of the individual.

"At Victor, people are motivated to give more than they otherwise give in this present society. This means they are motivated beyond simple financial need.

"In the authoritarian organization the goals are imposed from the top. At Victor, you have people working together at all different levels of the company and a man has a feeling that he is sharing in something. He is part of the goal determination and his self-esteem is involved. The pressure to do a better job comes from within the group and is accepted rather than being resented the way it is when it is imposed from the top. So you get greater productivity and this is true particularly outside the assembly line where, if people are motivated, they'll do something more than sit and shuffle papers.

"This pattern derives from the leadership. And what do you find when you look at A. C. Buehler? You see a guy who is getting a tremendous kick out of life, enjoying thoroughly what he is doing, just as a good ballplayer really enjoys the game.

"This is significant because it tends to imbue the organization with the same kind of excitement. The excitement of the game becomes a motivating factor. You look at what he has created about him and you find that he is staffed in depth. Alvin Bakewell is an extremely and unusually capable individual and Bert Buehler is a person who is extremely capable and is growing. Then on down through the organization, there's a formal structure. When I first saw Victor in 1961, it was almost unheard of for a company of Victor's size to have such a well-structured formal organization. Everybody's duties, responsibilities and accountability were set forth. A good organization requires a clear delineation of function and reporting because it is in this area where you get the most conflict, dissension and possible breakdown. Everything was written down. Everyone knew where he stood, so he could work at his own job and also he could work with everybody else without conflict.

"Victor had an excellent product line but more important was the whole management philosophy and the way people worked together. You had to say this company was a winner. You had to say that a combination of Comptometer with Victor would produce great benefits; two and two would equal more than four. And it has worked that way.

"The people who have had the capability have grown within this combined organization. They have been given opportunities

they never would have had—in terms of challenges, economic possibilities, a general enjoyment of life. And, of course, the shareholders have benefited. That's a matter of record."

This was the way Drexler, a practical and successful businessman with an academic background, saw Victor. How did A.C. look
at Comptometer? Just as you might expect from a man who gets
"a tremendous kick out of life." A.C. was well aware of the manifold problems at Comptometer. But it is very possible that if
there's anything A.C. enjoys more than a job well done, it's a problem. To him a problem is a challenge, an opportunity, and he
throws himself into the battle with single-minded purpose and
enthusiasm.

And there was an amazing fit to Comptometer and Victor. Of
course, the Comptometer machine itself fitted right into Victor's line of office figuring machines, a field that A.C. knew from
zero to nine to 9 million and 99. Used primarily for very high
volume work, the machine was not necessarily competitive with
Victor's products; rather, it broadened the product list. And in
that the major market for Comptometer was the large corporation,
Victor, the one-time specialist in the figuring problems of the small
businessman, was given added entree to big companies using all
kinds of figuring machines. Then, as a golfer and as a former manufacturer of golf carts, A.C. fully appreciated the possibilities for
growth in Comptometer's golf club and golf ball business. As
a matter of fact, A.C.'s interest in the leisure-time industries went
clear back to the 1920s when Victor briefly owned a motor boat
manufacturing company and A.C. delighted in driving in power
boat races. Comptometer's business forms division was not exactly
a stranger; A.C. was well aware of the proliferation of paper forms
in his own company and he had also been quite familiar with
McCaskey's carbon sales book, the grandaddy of modern business forms. It couldn't even be said that the Comptometer Schools

and temporary office help were foreign to A.C. and the Victor management; after all, the company always had been in the business of servicing the needs of offices, and it had its own sales and service network.

In any event, the name Victor Comptometer Corporation came into being on October 27, 1961, after approval of the merger terms by stockholders of both corporations. (Victor stockholder approval had been guaranteed in advance of the stockholders' meeting by A.C.) It was a $60,000,000-a-year operation with Victor contributing approximately twice the Comptometer volume—$40,000,000 to $20,000,000. Obviously, Victor would dominate in the formal and informal reorganization. Further, Victor's earnings record was conspicuously better than Comptometer's. Hence, it had been agreed that the 1,000,000 shares of Victor common stock would be converted into 3,600,000 shares. At the time of the merger, Comptometer had a little over 1,000,000 shares outstanding and these were exchanged share-for-share for the Victor stock, giving the combined company a total of approximately 4,600,000 common shares outstanding.

With the merger, Victor acquired Comptometer's listing, after due scrutiny, on the New York Stock Exchange (and a dual listing on the Pacific Coast Stock Exchange). In one jump, Victor had gone from private ownership to Big Board status. And with the public auction market establishing Victor's value, the company was suddenly worth $69,300,000. Not the combined companies, but Victor by itself. Of the total number of shares, 3,600,000 were Victor's and the stock was trading in the $19-a-share area. Yet the best offer A.C. had had when he was considering a public offering of Victor stock had been $18 a share with a total capitalization of 1,000,000 shares. With the merger, the market value of Victor was almost quadrupled and Comptometer was now in the corporate family, too. Perhaps most important were the problems and opportunities that arose.

"VCR" was the ticker symbol as first
sale of Victor Comptometer Corporation
stock was made at New York Stock
Exchange trading post on October 30,
1961. A. C. Buehler, Jr. (left) and Carl
Buehler III (right) study ticker tape with
Edward C. Gray, executive vice
president, New York Stock Exchange.

Theo L. Fox, now vice president for sales of the Business Machines Group, remembers some of it: "The merger wasn't final until the very end of October, 1961, and Bake was still in the hospital with a serious back ailment. When he did get back to work, A.C. asked him to handle the physical merger of the Comptometer and Victor sales forces. I was regional manager of the South Central region then, with headquarters in Dallas. Bake called all the regional managers into Chicago and we met with the general sales manager and his staff from Comptometer.

"We made preliminary plans on the basis of what we knew and what the Comptometer people knew about marketing areas and problems and about where individuals should go and where they would be most useful. Of course, a lot of this information was colored because the Comptometer people felt their man should be number one and the Victor people felt the same way. But Bake wanted the best men, up and down the line.

"We went back to the field and started in. In the four days before Christmas of 1961 and on through about the 5th of January, 1962, the five regional managers merged every Comptometer field office into a Victor office. We made the decisions on the locations of the offices and on the people. We selected people, rejected people, elevated people. I'd talk to the Comptometer man, perhaps, until one o'clock in the morning and then I'd talk to the Victor man until four o'clock in the morning and then I'd make my decision and go to the man and say, 'we're going with you.' Then I'd have to go back and take care of the other man. Then, off to another city. We sold off furniture, accounted for field inventory, determined who customers were, consolidated service records.

"I got caught in a snowstorm in Tulsa, Oklahoma on Christmas Eve day and I couldn't even phone home. I don't know how, but I talked my way on board a Convair and stood between Tulsa and Oklahoma City and somehow got on another Convair going to Dallas and got home something like a quarter to twelve midnight on Christmas Eve. We went back at it between Christmas and New Year's. We had our auditors out, a team of auditors assigned to each regional manager. The auditors would drop off and do their analysis and feed the information into Chicago and then hurry on to the next place. We had one regional manager who got three branches ahead of his auditors and he had to go back and go through a lot of the stuff again with the auditors to straighten out the chaos. But we got them all together in that time.

"Within a period of 15 days we had merged the whole damn thing. We did get around afterwards and polished it and made sure we had made the right moves. Yes, we did have a few people who felt they had been scratched, but we were able to go back and put iodine on and slap a bandage on and we were in business and we were going. In a period of less than 90 days in all, we had a functioning, going organization.

"I know of one corporation closely allied in our field that has had a merger in effect now for nine or ten years and it is still not a functioning, physical merger. If anyone wants to write a textbook about mergers, I think they ought to study the Victor-Comptometer merger as the example of how to do it."

And, as A.C. once commented, "You know, if you put the old New York Yankees in the golden days together with the worst team in the American League, some of the players on the cellar team would make it with the new team. That is, if anybody bothered to take a look at them and give them a chance. And Comptometer was far from the worst in the league. Probably the best single salesman we have came from Comptometer and we've got lots of their people doing fine jobs with us. There was resentment at first; you'd have to expect that, but we worked at bringing them in and I think things smoothed out pretty fast."

The annual report (for 1961) of Victor Comptometer Corporation showed A.C. hard at work in other areas:

The new members of the board of directors were Raymond J. Koch, former chairman of Comptometer; Lloyd Drexler, former vice chairman and chief executive officer; and Edward M. Cummings, a vice president of the Continental Illinois National Bank and Trust Company of Chicago, the company's long-time bank.

Raymond J. Koch was the newly appointed vice chairman and his son, Raymond F., was the corporate secretary. Otherwise there was no expansion of the top corporate structure. But Victor Comptometer had been reorganized categorically into distinct operating divisions: business machines, business forms, international, golf equipment, and electronics and research.

As rapidly as possible, the remaining office and factory force was being moved from Comptometer headquarters in Niles, Illinois and the old Comptometer buildings at 1735 North Paulina, Chicago (one of the Comptometer plants, built not too long after the turn of the century, was among the nation's first reinforced concrete buildings and had become an unofficial landmark building among architects). Even as the move was made, a $2,500,000 modernization and expansion program was well under way at the Victor home plant at 3900 North Rockwell. It was part of a $5,500,000 program of investment in a new plant and machinery begun in 1960.

Taking advantage of a contract clause, management got the company out from under the long-term payments called for under the Comptometer sale and leaseback arrangement. Buildings were repurchased and put up (successfully) for sale.

The earlier Comptometer decision to charge the heavy developmental expenses of the Electrowriter to future earnings was reversed. The annual report noted: "In order to avoid charging items against future earnings that related directly to past operations, and to conform to the accounting practices of Victor, charges amounting to $5,615,000 were made against retained earnings (or were shown as extraordinary charges in the earnings statement). The largest charge applied to the development costs and operating losses of the Electrowriter. These Electrowriter costs and losses had not been deducted from earnings up to October 31, 1961. In accordance with the accounting policy Comptometer Corporation had adopted, they had been deferred and were to be deducted from future earnings.

"These deferred charges amounted to $695,000 for the ten-month period of 1961 prior to the merger. The total deferred since the inception of the product was $3,457,000. To conform to the Victor policy of expensing all research and development costs, this entire amount has now been charged to retained earnings. Starting on November 1, 1961, Electrowriter operating results are being incorporated in current earnings."

Meanwhile, every division was being honed and polished, given financial assistance where needed, expanded in scope and manpower, and trained. It was hard, and, sometimes, slow work. But satisfying.

By the following year, first results were coming to the surface where they could be seen. Despite disruptions caused by the merger—plant closings, personnel changes, physical consolidations—and the time expended during special training courses for sales and management people, sales advanced five percent in 1962, reaching $63,300,000. The profits picture was less easy to measure, but the important point was that earnings were up.

Comptometer had brought with it a tax loss carry-forward which radically altered final earnings for several years, and then too, there were the extraordinary charges of 1961, making comparisons difficult. In 1961, with the tax loss carry-forward available to the combined corporation for only two months, Victor Comptometer earned $4,678,000 before federal income tax. After income taxes of $1,673,000, but before extraordinary charges, net earnings for 1961 were $3,010,000, equivalent to 65 cents a share. In 1962, the company earned $5,018,000 before paying a nominal income tax of $101,000. Hence, with no extraordinary charges, net income was $4,917,000, equal to $1.06 per common share.

Meanwhile, new sales offices had been opened, bringing the total of direct company branch offices to 68 and the large-scale sales and service training program had been completed so that every salesman was equipped to sell the Comptometer products and the full Victor line of adding machines and calculators. The late model Victor electric calculators with their expanded capacity, plus the excellent contacts of the Comptometer sales organization in major corporations, meant that at last Victor had made the transition from a company offering a $100 adding machine to the corner grocer to a corporation offering the widest and fullest variety of machines to all segments of the market, the corner store to the billion-dollar giant.

And A.C. was watching the growth of the computer carefully, both as it affected industry sales and as it might dictate corporate policy. In the 1962 annual report, he commented:

"The markets for Victor business machines have been greatly expanded by the increasing use of computers and of automated production equipment which is tied in with computers. Whenever a company uses a computer, there is a tremendously increased need for the preparation of input data as well as for the analysis of processed data. Significantly, some of the best customers for Victor's business machines are major American corporations which have pioneered in the development of our computer economy.

"The anticipated growth in the use of computers gives some indication of the potential markets for other business machines. To date, approximately 14,000 electronic computers have been installed ... (But) at the end of 1962, there were more computers on order than the entire total presently installed. While the related demand for Victor business machines is not expected to increase this fast, it is clear that the demand for electronic computers provides Victor with an expanding market."

A. C. could see the computer affecting Victor's operation in other significant ways. With computers spewing out data in unbelievable amounts on high-speed printers, a billion-dollar market was being created for specially-adapted forms that could be fed through the printers. Victor management looked over the properties it had acquired—plants in Lincoln, Nebraska; Arlington, Texas; and Passaic, New Jersey. It closed the unprofitable Passaic plant and started on a program of expansion. The separate business forms companies had been reorganized and put under a new central staff headquartered in Lincoln, Nebraska, and a new $1,750,000 plant was under construction at Lincoln. In the Victor tradition of investing in the best of equipment, it would replace an antiquated and inefficient plant and boast the latest in high-speed, offset printing presses.

Through acquisitions in the next year, it acquired the commercial printing and business forms operations of Cullom & Ghertner of Nashville, Tennessee and Atlanta, Georgia, and the D. C. Wooden Co. of Kalamazoo, Michigan. In 1964, Victor acquired Redi-Rite Business Forms, Inc. of San Francisco, California and subsequently built a new plant in Merced, California to replace its leased San Francisco facility, and one in Kalamazoo to replace an outmoded leased facility there.

The computer was the symbol of the automated industrial society of the future. In A.C.'s view, that future meant more leisure time and more leisure-time activity for increasing numbers as the work week shrank.

Thus golf, one of the fastest growing of all leisure activities, offered Victor unusual opportunity. The Worthington Ball Company Division was combined with the Burke Golf Equipment Division and put under single management with headquarters in

Morton Grove, a Chicago suburb. After all, golf balls and clubs are sold through the same channels, so there was no reason to keep the companies separate. A decision was made to add another manufacturing facility for golf clubs with the best of manufacturing equipment at the Morton Grove plant, once occupied by the old Victor Electri-Car company.

The golf division was also strengthened with the purchase of the Des Moines Glove and Mfg. Co. and its sales subsidiary, the Tufhorse Co. The acquisition enabled Victor to add to its ball and club line one of the best known golf bags, as well as accessories like club covers, shag bags, and carryalls.

Looking the corporation over, gold was found in unlikely places. For instance, the corporation was saddled with a long-term lease on a fancy headquarters building Comptometer had taken on in suburban Niles, Illinois. It developed that the Rauland Corporation, a subsidiary of the Zenith Corporation, was interested in the building. Victor quickly bought the building from the owner, the Greyhound Corporation, and just as quickly resold it to Zenith. Victor was out from under an annual occupancy cost of $250,000. More and more, it was looking like a streamlined organization.

And a substantial and increasing return was showing up from an unexpected but not neglected source. Reorganized and expanded under a new banner, the Comptometer Schools and the Victor Temporaries were prospering. Founded in 1905 to teach clerical help (strictly male in the early years) how to use the Comptometer, the schools were now teaching other office skills. The schools offered help to their graduates in obtaining a first job, a service which almost forced the schools into the business of supplying businesses with temporary office help. Now, in the 1960s, in a time of increasing labor shortages, temporary help was in strong demand. By 1967, Victor was making the school and temporary help services available in some 77 different locations across the

United States and Canada.

With its big earning power, Victor used up the last of the Comptometer tax loss carry-forward in 1963 and paid a substantial federal income tax. Thus, while pretax earnings increased more than half a million dollars to $5,546,000, net after taxes was down to $4,055,000, equal to 88 cents a share.

To the unsophisticated, the bare bones figures—88 cents a share in 1963 versus $1.06 in 1962—may have made it look as if Victor Comptometer was losing ground. But, with sales up to almost $66,000,000, the truth was that the company was making solid progress. If the earnings had been fully taxed in both years, the company would have made 59 cents a share in 1962 and would have shown a healthy increase to 67 cents in 1963.

Perhaps as important as anything else was the news that the Electrowriter had reached, for all practical purposes, a break-even point, with profits apparently ahead. In fact, the division was in the black for the second half of the year and was able to wipe out all but $5,000 of the loss run up in the first half. Only two years earlier, the operation had lost $1,100,000.

The Comptometer, and the broad line of Victor machines were now being sold in 68 domestic direct branches and by representatives in 712 additional cities. More than 4,000 dealers around the country were also selling Victor's fledgling line of cash registers and its inexpensive Champion brand adding machines. International sales were strong (sales up six percent in 1963). Business machines were being sold through 141 sales outlets in a total of 71 countries.

And for the first time, another Victor project was being heard from. For years, in addition to its continuing interest in the electronic digital computer, Victor had been concerned with the digital computer's little known step-brother, the analog computer. In fact, the Victor-made Norden bombsight of World War II was

"Communication leads to understanding" was the message handwritten by A. C. Buehler on a Victor Electrowriter and transmitted via the communications satellite Telstar to a receiving unit a few feet away. This October 18, 1962 communication was the first handwritten message to and from outer space.

by definition an analog computer. So, too, was the test system built by Victor to check the Convair B-58 Hustler. During flight, 576 different measurements—temperatures, pressures, speed and acceleration marks, and structural stresses—were picked up by sensing devices and translated (the analog) into readable data. Now Victor was confining itself to the manufacture of a read-out assembly for use by others who made analog computers and other sensing and measuring systems. This was Digit-Matic. The unit consists of lead-in cables and terminals and a solenoid system fitted to the keys of standard or specially designed Victor figuring machines. A system manufactured and sold, for instance, by Nuclear-Chicago Corporation monitors radiation, sending electronic impulses to a Digit-Matic unit where the solenoids trip appropriate keys and a digital print-out is automatically and continuously created for the information of technicians. The applications are many and varied in industry, business, research, the military. One unusual application: Motorola's Alarm Reporting Systems uses the Digit-Matic unit in a plant protection system; the print-out in a central guard station will show that door number 127 or gate number 4 is being opened.

In 1963, Digit-Matic sales jumped an even 30 percent. The company was able to predict a "very good market for these units as long as people want to list out numbers; we offer a very reliable, simple, and inexpensive way of listing numbers from data processing equipment."

It was in 1963 that another (and final) move was made to clean up leftover housekeeping problems. Through a national group of investment banking houses headed by Glore, Forgan & Co. (now Glore Forgan, Wm. R. Staats Inc.), Victor Comptometer raised nearly $15,000,000 through an offering of debentures. Proceeds from the 4⅞ percent sinking fund debentures, due 1988, were used for working capital and to retire the company's long-

term and current indebtedness, including $1,711,000 of 6½ per-
cent debentures originally issued by Comptometer. In all, Victor
paid off $10,797,000, almost all of it, except for $3,350,000, accu-
mulated by Comptometer. The $3,350,000 represented bank bor-
rowings by Victor for the expansion and modernization of the
company plant and offices.

With the debt consolidated and put on a long-term basis, with
new capital to build growth, with sales up and real earnings improving, the board of directors voted the first cash dividend of the
combined Victor Comptometer Corporation. The dividend, five
cents a share, was made payable January 15, 1964. Later, the directors agreed to put the five-cent dividend on a regular quarterly
basis. The future looked good.

CHAPTER 11

"Give a Man a Yardstick"

A housewife would appreciate it. So would an efficiency expert. The cleaning people, vacuuming, scrubbing or waxing the floors of the Victor home offices, are relieved of one time-consuming and annoying task. They don't have to pick up wastebaskets, move them aside, clean the floor where the basket was, and then return the basket to its original place. The wastebaskets are hung a half foot off the floor on the side of the desks where, incidentally, they are very handy for the user.

It may be a detail, but it is a striking example of the very attention to detail that not only helps to make the entire company, office and factory, remarkably efficient, but also a more pleasant place to work.

A leader since its earliest day in the art and the science of mass producing the interchangeable part for mass production assembly, Victor Comptometer in its 50th anniversary year is still refining and extending its expertise in production. George Bullen, vice president—manufacturing for the Business Machines Group, is fond of saying that the secret of Victor's success is its far-flung and effective sales force. Alvin Bakewell, the architect of that sales organization and now president of the corporation, says the heart of the matter is the factory's efficiency and high morale. Both may be equally correct, but in any event, the company has come a long way since the "you-make-them, I'll-sell-them. No, you-sell-them, I'll-make-them" days. There's respect on all sides, easy communication, and a smooth working relationship.

One of Bullen's most recent Christmas presents, he says, was two sizable orders turned in by the Victor International sales force. Both were new accounts. One came from Japan, the other from Italy. As with all Victor sales, foreign and domestic, the machines to fill the Japanese and Italian orders were manufactured in the 3900 North Rockwell plant in Chicago and were shipped from there. Now selling in 77 nations, Victor is the only company in its field that successfully does a volume foreign business without the need of overseas manufacturing plants. Victor's remarkable success in selling Chicago-made machines in the teeth of the stiffest world competition is indicated by the size of its Japanese sales company: 160 salesmen in 16 offices in Japan.

With specific examples from related fields well in mind, George Bullen comments: "Victor today produces units at the rate of 300,000 a year—one machine every 10 seconds during the working day—in the same amount of space and with the same employees that would produce fewer than 100,000 units if the manufacturing methods were not up to date. Or, to put it another way, if we were using the older methods and machinery, we would need three times our present space to meet our present production schedules."

The Chicago plant space is about 525,000 square feet. One-location production has many obvious advantages; duplicate tooling is avoided, manufacturing equipment is fully utilized, rigid quality control can be maintained, and minor changes in a particular model can be made with the full research-engineering-production-service-marketing team participating. Then changes do not need to be duplicated on other production-assembly lines.

Communication is excellent and virtually instant. The director of product engineering has his office on one side of the production headquarters room. On the other side, next to each other, are the offices of the directors of quality control, of industrial engineering, and of production control. In between these three and the product engineering director are the people who work with them. Everybody concerned with a problem or a decision is immediately available. "That includes A.C. and Bake and Bert; their doors are always open and you can get an answer," Bullen says, adding:

"This is not a committee company. We pretty well believe in the old saw that a camel is a horse constructed by a committee. We do have regular staff meetings, of course, to maintain our communications. But they are short and to the point, no idle conversation. We know what we're going to talk about, we get at it, and next meeting we get an action report. We have quality assurance meetings once a week for each of the product lines. All departments are represented at each meeting. That includes someone from the service department; if there are any problems in the field we hear about it right away. The calculator is the biggest product line so we have that meeting at 4:30 in the afternoon. When you start a meeting at 4:30, all the baloney gets cut out of it right away."

Born in 1911, the son of Baptist missionaries, Bullen is a University of Maine graduate in electrical engineering. He came to Victor after years of manufacturing and administrative experience with General Electric and Remington Rand and World War II duty as a major in charge of a tank rebuilding plant. At Victor Comptometer, Bullen appreciates the willingness of the board of directors and of top management to invest in the latest and best machinery.

"We don't just replace a machine," Bullen says. "If a punch press is due for replacement, we don't merely buy another one like it, or even the company's latest and improved model. We search the world to see if there's a better machine on the market even when it is for a routine job. Or we see if we can suggest changes to a manufacturer that would improve the efficiency of the machine. We build some of our own equipment and we're always working with manufacturers on theirs. We take a look at the job and the machine and try to figure if it can be eliminated. If not, isn't there an entirely different way of doing the job, using entirely different machinery?

"It is a continuing program everybody has a hand in from the top down. Everybody's suggestions are welcome and discussed. The men on the line take a real interest. All kinds of ideas come in through the suggestion program and the work simplification program and the people are recognized for their contributions. But we also have an organized program under the direction of a manager for machinery and equipment. He goes outside for ideas, too, attends the machinery shows, reviews publications, and talks to manufacturers.

"We want the best machinery and the best value for our money.

(1)

(2)

(3)

(4)

Victor production efficiency is illustrated
by (1) bank of automatic punch presses,
(2) automatic pin-setting machine,
(3) 10-stage automatic riveting machine,
(4) electrostatic die-making machine, and
(5) coordinate measuring machine for
maintaining quality control of purchased
parts. Through the years, Victor became
a high-production manufacturer in a
traditionally low-production industry.

(5)

If we can back up what we recommend, we're pretty sure to get what we want. I'd say that top management here is as conscious as any in the country of the true value to the corporation of the manufacturing operation. You know, some companies think they are doing great when they bleed production dry. They save money on capital investment but they end up with low output and very high-cost production. They lose out not only on unit volume but also on quality and on the cost of scrap and rework. On the other hand, we don't junk a machine just because it happens to be written off the books. We'll use it as long as we can use it effectively."

As might be expected on the basis of Victor's record of far-sighted management, advanced and automated machinery has been phased in at the Rockwell Street plant with a minimum of friction.

When it comes to the introduction of radical and labor-saving equipment, Victor management does as it has in other matters where employee interests are at stake. It communicates. It involves the employees in the project. It recognizes employee interests. It compensates as reason dictates. Specifically, as far in advance as possible (a year, even two years), employees are told about the machine, about what it will mean for the employees and what it will accomplish for the corporation. Suggestions are sought. No one loses a job. Normal attrition and transfers, with retraining where necessary to equal or better jobs, take care of the displacement problem. Employees are interviewed individually on whether they wish to stay and operate the new machine or transfer to other work. And individually and plant-wide, employees participate in increased productivity.

Examples are abundant in Victor's clean, well-lighted, and well-organized plant, both in parts fabrication and in assembly. Victor adding machines and calculators contain an average of 2,300 parts and the parts fabrication lines turn out upwards of 2,760,000 parts each working day to supply the assembly line. About 200,000 out of that daily total is accounted for by springs, the tiny springs that provide the proper degree of tension for the keys and other mechanisms inside the machines. Prior to 1963, the spring itself—or the dozens of varieties of springs—was produced by machines. But the tiny loops at each end of the spring, used to attach the spring in position, were formed by hand. Then the Sleeper-Hartley Co. developed a machine that would do the looping operation automatically and the U. S. Baird Machine Co. produced a machine that would automatically generate a complete spring. A Victor supervisor recalls: "The girls were told about them at once. When the first machine was received at the plant, it was demonstrated for the girls. They were enthusiastic about it and were quite willing to be transferred to other jobs. They thought it was good for Victor and I'm sure they weren't forgetting the Victor profit-sharing plan in which all employees participate. We were able, as we'd put it, to release 40 girls for other work in the plant."

Victor was a pioneer in the use of powdered metal to fabricate parts. In the ordinary machining, stamping and forging of a part, a finishing process is needed and there's usually waste metal. In modern powdered metal technology, an exact measure of metal in powder form is sifted into a die and then compacted. The compacting pressure is tremendous, pressing the powder into a solid. The part—a wheel, a sprocket, a gear—is kicked out and sent through a heat treatment (sintering). The compacting process is automatic, continuous and high-speed. The machines require only supervision. Varying the ingredients of the powder and controlling the sintering process produces different alloys and different finishes. There are many other advantages, e.g., two or more parts that are ordinarily made as separate pieces and then assembled may be made as one piece.

Most companies using the process compact the part, sinter and then restrike and resinter, but Victor-inspired improvements in the technology allow Victor to get the same quality and strength in a single cycle. Particularly with the Victor advances, says George Bullen, "the savings are tremendous." Some 60 different Victor parts are now made of powdered metal and the total output of powdered metal parts exceeds 3,000,000 a month.

Then there's the Hill-Rockford riveter made in Rockford, Illinois. Previously, an operator positioned a piece and pressed a foot lever. Pressure of the foot lever controlled the force and the duration of the riveting action. For the next rivet, possibly smaller, a different pressure and time cycle was needed. Training was long. Now with the Hill-Rockford riveter, the piece is positioned and set up for as many as six to ten rivets. Once tripped, the machine bangs in the rivets in succession at exactly the right pre-set force and duration.

The list is long and the accomplishments many, but George Bullen is the first to say that the Victor men and women—and the attitude they have—are more important than the machines. "We want each one to feel that he is a necessary part of the team. The simplest operations are important. Each of us is helping to build machines. New employees are given a tour of the entire plant so they can see the end products and all the steps it takes to complete them. They are carefully instructed on the job they are to perform. The importance of their job to the completion of a quality Victor product is also stressed."

The company works at it, and always has. As A.C. once said: "You can measure a Mickey Mantle. You can find out how much he weighs and how tall he is and how good his eyesight is and you can measure his strength in a number of ways. But until he performs, until he produces results, you can't measure his motivation. That may be most important of all. You've seen what happens sometimes when they switch managers between seasons or during a season. The club just takes off. Now, no matter what else, this new manager is able to motivate the very same men to give out as individuals and also to work as a team."

A reading on how well A.C. and his assistants have done in building and holding together a loyal team can be seen in the dozens of veterans at Victor. And in the number of second-generation employees and the father-son combinations and husband-wife teams. The Old-Timers Club, which enjoys a dinner dance and awards presentation with A.C. and his wife every year, is made up of employees who have been with Victor's Business Machines Group for 20 years or more. The membership now totals over 400.

Victor morale, of course, flows from A.C. and his personal philosophy. But the implementation is there in broad policy and in detailed administration. A few years back, the president of a corporation listed among the nation's top 500 was talking about management technique. "I'd pay $1,000,000 for A. C. Buehler's black book," he said.

Actually, A.C. does not have a "black book"; he has a series of books, bound in different colors, the colors following an established code keyed to different subsidiaries and activities. One set of books establishes the structure of the company, defining duties and responsibilities, and the flow of information and decision-making authority. The other volumes systematically provide constantly updated information on the operations of the company, carried down to the smallest possible profit centers.

A.C.'s million-dollar set of directives starts with A.C.: "Subject: Chairman, Victor Comptometer Corporation. (Paragraph 1), Basic Function: The Chairman is the chief executive officer of the corporation, responsible for providing the proper administration in all aspects of the corporation's activities to insure the realization of maximum profits and growth compatible with the best interests of employees, consumers, and shareholders . . .

A. C. Buehler presents service awards at
the annual Victor Old Timers Club
dinner dance and awards presentation.
The membership is made up of
employees who have been with Victor's
Business Machines Group 20 years or
more and totals more than 400.

"(Paragraph 7) Account number. The salary of the Chairman, staff members and clerical assistants under his direct supervision are to be charged to Account #810, followed by an expense account number . . ."

Everyone from the chairman on down knows the broad outlines of his job and is given freedom within those outlines to function as best he can. "It is good to give a man a yardstick by which he can measure himself," says A.C., instead of beating on him from above to do a better job." Then, too, job definition imparts a sense of organization and of the individual's place in the organization.

Vincent G. McDonagh, Victor's treasurer, comments: "A.C. designed and developed the controls in use in the company. This in itself is highly unusual; you wouldn't find many corporate chairmen or presidents with the knowledge and grasp necessary to set up a working system of internal accounting controls. In addition to his built-in ESP, A.C. really controls things through these accounting records. All the records are uniform in design, making it possible for top management to see easily and quickly what is going on.

"A.C. and the corporate officers get a flash report of sales and profits of each group and division on the 8th or 10th of each month. The flash report shows the current figures against the same figures a year earlier and against the forecast. A more detailed monthly report follows. The forecast is prepared each month for the 12 months ahead and it projects cash needs as well as sales and earnings probabilities for each group and division."

Once a series of interviews with relatively new Victor employees uncovered an alarming belief that plant foremen were incompetent, didn't know their jobs. Investigation by the conscientious personnel department headed by Bertram W. Lawrenz pinpointed the source of the very mistaken impression: this being Victor, the supervisors all had well-trained and competent assistants; when a new man reported for work, the foreman would turn him over to the proper assistant for job orientation and instruction; thus came the idea that while the fellows down the line were cracker-jack, the boss was lacking. The foremen were immediately tipped off and asked to shoulder more of the orientation. A follow-up survey indicated that the supervisors were getting the high marks they deserved from the men.

In few corporations, large or small, is there such constant and intimate communication between management and employee. Contact is formal and informal. Any day (or night) A.C. or Bakewell or Bert Buehler or George Bullen can be found out on the factory floor looking and listening and feeling the beat of a plant at work, stopping to ask after Bill's ailing wife or Joe's first baseman son. Once during a plant remodeling, A.C. reluctantly approved plans for an executive dining room. Even before the room was opened, A.C. decided that it would be used only for entertaining guests. But even that went against the grain for A.C. "I think the board of directors used the room once," a Victor officer recalls, "and since then it has been used for meetings." A.C. and all the other officers push their own trays through the cafeteria line and sit wherever there's an empty table.

Among the formal channels of communications, there's the "anniversary interview." The personnel department keeps track of the employment date of every employee. Each year on that date the employee is asked to stop by the personnel office for a chat with one of the trained men on the staff.

Personnel Director Lawrenz comments: "Basically, the purpose is to find out if the man has any gripes and if there's anything we can do to help him and if he's doing anything to help himself. Interviews will last anywhere from 5 to 15 minutes. Sometimes we uncover some really rankling problem. We always ask first if the man has talked to his supervisor. Often he hasn't. He may think the supervisor is too busy to bother with such a problem. If the man's willing, we'll call the supervisor right then and get him down here and have the problem right out.

"Then the interviews are very helpful in terms of promotions. We try to promote from within wherever possible. It is our responsibility to recognize ability and education. A person's job is a good part of his life. If you put him in the wrong place under the wrong conditions, you can make his whole life miserable and that of his family, too. It is the employee's responsibility to do his best on the job and it is our responsibility to recognize what he's doing. The company encourages people to take training courses and college courses and we'll help pay for them. Often we can give a man advice on what and where to study, and if he's studying and doing good work, we can help him here. We'll take a look at his work and then we'll flip a note up to the employment office saying, for instance, next time you need to hire a draftsman, please consider Tom Brown in the shipping department."

In all this, A.C. has definite ideas about what he is trying to achieve. He comments:

"You try a little harder for your people and you get a little more back. What's worth more than all the machinery and equipment and bricks and mortar is the spirit of the people. By that I mean the feeling that people like what they're doing, that they want to be good at it, and that they want the company to be good at it. The personnel department does a good job. A lot of our people, after they've been here a while, will take their problems, even their personal problems, to the department. You know, a fellow can't seem to get along with his wife. Or the daughter is getting married and, of course, the guy's a bum. That happens in every family. So we give them a chance to talk and try to give them some good counsel. It is good when the men feel enough confidence to bring their troubles in.

"You know, people don't go around carrying signs on their backs saying 'I'm qualified for a better job.' You have to keep looking them over, studying them, finding out what they want to do and what they are preparing themselves for. You have to dig these things out. A lot of people are shy or modest. And you can't wait until there's a job opening or a promotion to be filled and then start looking under the desks or in the closets. We note these things down on the job records along with what a man's supervisor says and anything else that might be helpful in moving him along.

"Another thing, I've always said if you want to prevent yourself from getting a better job, just let it be known that there's no one who can fill your job. If we move you into another job and there really isn't anyone to do your job, then we have to hire somebody off the street and train him. In the better job, you'll need some period of training at least. So why not hire somebody from the outside in the first place and train him for the better job. That way, only one man needs training.

"But if a man comes in and says he'd like to try something new and explains that Joe in the department can do his job just as well as he can, you're free to let him move. He's trying and you ought to give him a chance.

"In the factory, down on the assembly line, we try to teach the people more than one operation. If there's a change in production methods, or if somebody is sick, you can shift people around. So we do cross training, teaching people to handle two and three jobs. We have different assembly lines for different machines—the simple adder to the electric calculator and so forth—and they require different skills. Then, on each line there are jobs that require greater and lesser skills. Our cross training will also give a man a chance to move up the line to a better paying job. Then, too, the training a man takes outside is considered when promotions are made and merit raises given."

The merit raise is the heart of the payment system at Victor. Philosophically, the company is opposed to the general wage increase, handed out willy-nilly to all and sundry. On occasion, plant-wide increases have been necessary to make certain that the general wage level remained in its historic and leading relationship with area wages. For instance, before Christmas of 1966, Bert Buehler surprised the plant in a talk over the public address system by volunteering a five percent general wage increase. It was apparent to the Victor management that the federal administration's wage-price guidelines were crumbling and the 1967 wages would inflate. But for the most part, Victor depends on the individual merit increase to provide monetary rewards.

Every job in the plant is classified and assigned a range of possible payments starting with a basic hiring rate and moving upward. Recommendations from supervisors and a review of the job records meticulously maintained by the personnel department determine how fast and how far up the pay ladder an employee may move. The new Victor employee shortly finds himself sprucing up his personal appearance if need be, watching such things as paper or scrap material on the floors, and making sure he carries his own weight on the job, all without being told or ordered.

Another noteworthy factor in Victor employee relations is the assurance that no one is discharged capriciously. According to A.C., "We want to make sure if anybody is dismissed around here, we know why. Anybody that we release for poor performance, absenteeism, chronic lateness, or things of that sort, must have a notation on the back of his record. If it isn't on the back of that record, there isn't anyone who can fire him. Now, if he punches a foreman or something like that, that's something else. But normally, we have to have three formal complaints entered before an employee is dismissed and when a foreman comes in here with a charge we ask if he's talked to the man or woman. We want to make sure he has a chance to air his grievances, too, if he has any."

In terms of bringing the employee into the picture and in terms of doing the job well, little is as important at Victor as its long-time work simplification program. A formal program was instituted in 1957. Organized, structured group sessions are held on a continuing basis to consider specific jobs, methods and systems and to uncover ways of accomplishing the same or additional work more efficiently. From top management on down the line, participants have found the free and open discussions stimulating and helpful. "I would say," comments A.C., "that if anybody should know how to do a job better, or faster, it would be the man who is working on it every day. We give them examples of what's happened in the past, times when someone has made a change or thought of something that made the work simpler and easier. And then we set up the problem and try to consider it from scratch and we get down to all the little things finally—maybe if we turned the part this way or that way in the press, we could get a little more speed. Everybody gets his chance to have his say. The meetings encourage people to think, to plan. Many employees may tend to think there's nothing in it for them in increasing output. They just come in and do the job and go home in some companies. But this program gives them an idea of what's going on and a feeling that they can do better if the company does better.

"It's amazing what can come out of these meetings, what people think of. Some of the ideas are so simple you wonder where we've been for the last 40 years. I really mean it. It's amazing. We don't pay directly for the ideas that may be developed in these meetings. It's a group effort. We do have a full suggestion program and we pay one-sixth of the net savings over a year for any suggestion that is adopted. We've had excellent results from both programs in terms of money-saving ideas and our people know that making things go along better will be reflected in their pay enve lopes. They learn that quickly. Still the big benefits for us and for the people is that we let them in on it, let them know what's going on. Then you get people who are trying to go the same way you are going."

The Victor work simplification program, based on the thinking developed by industrial engineer Allan H. Mogensen and taught at his Lake Placid conferences, was of special value as the company worked hard in the years following the merger with Comptometer to build a smoothly functioning and efficient organization.

CHAPTER 12

Products for Many Markets

"Someone once told me," A.C. recalls, "that when you acquire another company it takes one full year for management to learn the new business, one year to set the goals of the combined company and two years to implement those plans. Finally, in the fifth year, you start getting results."

A.C., it would appear, ran well ahead of that schedule in putting Comptometer together with Victor even though Comptometer was a diverse and troubled company at the time the merger was completed late in 1961. The sales of the two companies for that year added up to $60,486,000, while the profits before taxes came to $4,678,000. By 1965, the fourth full year of Victor management of the combined company, sales had boomed to $88,767,000 and before-tax profits had leaped to $9,862,000. And, in 1966, that fifth year when "you start getting results," Victor Comptometer sales topped the one hundred million dollar mark at $104,172,000 and pre-tax profits were a very impressive $16,735,000. Of all U. S. manufacturing companies, Victor Comptometer was then the 583rd largest in ranking by total sales. Within its industry classification—office, computing and accounting machines—a classification led by International Business Machines and studded with names like Xerox, the company showed the third best ratio of current assets to liabilities, the second best profit in relation to stockholder equity.

Seventy-nine percent of corporate sales were coming out of the business machine products and services handled by the Business Machines Group and International Group, and a healthy share of the big increases were also being produced by the same Groups. There were reasons: Victor Comptometer was now offering the industry's broadest line of adding machines and calculators. The line included more than 75 basic models, led by the new Premier Calculators, 10-key fully automatic machines.

At the same time, Victor was opening up a noteworthy new market. Recognizing the needs—and the affluence—of the householder in this age of credit and mandatory record keeping for everything from income taxes to check book accounting, Victor introduced the Tallymaster, a small, 10-key decorator-designed series of machines priced at a level that would make sense to husband and wife harassed by mounting home paperwork.

While the complete line of figuring machines was being sold in

1967 through 84 company-owned branch offices and through some 700 factory-trained sales and service representatives, approximately 6,000 dealers were selling Victor's low-priced Champion line, intended for small business.

Victor, having been conceived in 1918 out of an idea for a compact, inexpensive figuring machine for the corner store, was not only still doing business at the same stand, but also was doing more business there than ever.

And "results" were coming in thick and fast from other sectors of the company. For years, going back to the days of the McCaskey merger and possibly even before that, A.C. had been intrigued by the vast market for cash registers and he had been determined that Victor would step strongly into that market, dominated for decades by National Cash Register. But, as Victor developed through the years, the hour never seemed to materialize when it would have been wise to have diverted major time, energy and money to the effort. Over the years, the McCaskey adding machine with cash drawer had become the Series 9 line of Victor cash registers. But despite expansions, improvements and new models, the line was still meant for smaller business establishments with fairly simple requirements in the way of separate tallies for different clerks and different kinds of merchandise.

In 1966, the problem was solved by a leapfrogging step. After a series of transatlantic meetings and negotiations, a long-term agreement was signed with Hugin Kassaregister A.B., a prominent Swedish manufacturer, under which Victor would market Hugin cash registers in the United States and Canada.

At the time, A.C. commented: "Hugin's cash registers are regarded as sophisticated equipment and are highly respected for quality and durability throughout the free world." The key phrase was "sophisticated equipment."

Victor was now ready to make its move in the cash register

market, which is estimated to represent about $200,000,000 in annual sales. It was able to offer models to meet virtually every conceivable need of a retailer. The process of recruitment and training of additional specialized sales and service personnel began and supply lines were beginning to be filled.

The results from the Electrowriter, the fascinating long-distance handwriting machine which had been inherited from Comptometer, are recalled with some pride and amusement by Victor's president, Alvin Bakewell:

"The year we took over Comptometer, they had a loss on the Electrowriter of $1,100,000. We said that in the second year we'd bring the loss down to a half million dollars and that we'd come close to breaking even in the third year. There for a while it got to be a kind of a joke in the board of directors meeting. Someone would say, 'Why don't you ditch the thing?' or 'Why don't you sell it off? It is just a drain.' And I'd say 'No, we're going to make some money out of it.' So in the second year—the first year we had it—we did bring the losses down to half a million and in the third year we lost 5,000-odd dollars. After that, we made money every year.

"It was about a $3,000,000 business in 1966 and it is going up. We're getting more units out, we brought down the manufacturing cost and we made some major improvements. And we switched the emphasis from leasing to outright sales, bringing more cash in and cutting down on the financing costs."

The great utility of the Electrowriter is that it offers an inexpensive way to transmit information, instructions and diagrams from one to another (or to any number of points), providing a permanent record at both ends. No "input" machine is needed and anyone who can write can operate the unit. An airlines clerk can pick up the electronic pen and scribble "J. Jones, first class, flight 101," and the reservations people at computer center in-

Early-day McCaskey register (above) consisted of a Victor-made adding machine on top of a cash drawer. These machines were the forerunners of Victor's current cash register line. Series 40 (left) meets requirements of high-volume outlets.

stantly have the record. A floor nurse can "write" to the admission desk that Room 896 has been vacated. A weather forecaster can draw in the cloud cover or the wind direction on a prepared weather map for the information of the tower, the pilot ready room, the operations officer.

The potential of the Electrowriter is indicated by the breakdown of the markets designated by the sales organization. They are: public utilities; hotels-motels; transportation (trucks, airlines, railroads, buses); retail-wholesale; steel and primary metals; food, chemical and other processing; general manufacturing; financial services; hospitals and clinics; general services; building materials; and government—federal, state, and local. And to serve these many markets, Victor has established a separate direct sales organization with offices in 28 major cities.

Finally, with the exception of the military and the federal and private weather services, there's the biggest single market for the Electrowriter. This is education. And VERB.

VERB stands for Victor Electrowriter Remote Blackboard. The system ties an Electrowriter transmitter to receivers by direct lines or by long-distance telephone lines. A projection unit picks up the material on the receivers and projects it on a screen. Thus, any number of students see the blackboard illustrations of a highly qualified instructor as he lectures over the audio part of the system. Carbon County, Wyoming offers one example of the use of VERB. The system is installed in six high schools with instruction beamed from a center at Sinclair, Wyoming to schools in such towns as Rawlins, Baggs, Saratoga, Hanna, Encampment and Medicine Bow.

By the end of 1967, Victor management had built a new and substantial division out of what had been for more than half a century a subsidiary operation at Comptometer—the schools set up around the country to train Comptometer operators. Through

77 offices in the United States and Canada under the banner of the Victor Better Business Services, the company was offering some or all of these services: training in the operation not only of Victor and Comptometer machines, but also of sophisticated accounting machines; peripheral computer equipment such as keypunch machines; a calculating service for companies overloaded with high volume work; and temporary office help. The comments of Bert Buehler regarding Victor's Better Business Services are interesting for what they reveal about Victor and for what they say about the changing needs of business in an era of continuing shortages of qualified people.

"At the time of the merger, top management at Victor decided they would separate this collateral Comptometer operation—the schools—from sales and service where it had been and put it on its own and see if it could sustain itself and pay a profit. The foundation was the Comptometer Schools, which went back to 1905. From 1905 to 1952, there was not much change in the program. Then management decided that as long as they had the machines and the personnel, they might as well try to offer a calculating service. Today we're in this in a big way. We figure store inventories on a regional basis for J. C. Penney Company, for instance, and we do inventory work for Western Auto; we do lots of special, big jobs like figuring election returns and we do as well as or better than the computers.

"As a natural sideline, Comptometer had entered into the employment field and did supply Comptometer operators on a temporary help basis. In 1960 it was decided to expand into temporary help all the way—stenographers, typists, bookkeepers, or what have you—in the office field.

"But at the time of the merger it was a frail operation and many of the schools were sick. We had to perform a pruning operation and we closed 12 schools right off the bat. Many people thought it

Comptometer Schools (top) offer training in the operation of figuring machines, business arithmetic, key-punch skills, and general office procedure. Victor's full range of temporary office help (center) and special calculating services (lower) stemmed from Comptometer Schools, which trace back to 1905.

was a useless effort, but we were paying our own way by the end of 1962 and we got healthy in 1963 and 1964. Today this is a multi-million dollar business and we showed a substantial growth from 1966 to 1967. We've been opening new offices all over—Seattle, San Antonio, Anaheim, San Jose, Memphis. We have something unusual here—we have schools all across the United States and Canada, we have the biggest single calculating service in the country and we are a growing factor in diversified temporary help. They all tie in together, and there even may be a public relations side effect that helps in the sales of our figuring machines.

"It is interesting to note that the temporary help industry today is rated anywhere from a quarter of a billion to a half of a billion dollars annually. The Institute for Temporary Services has even estimated that if you include all phases of temporary help—salesmen and unskilled labor among others—it might go as high as a billion dollars a year. So this is a tremendous industry and, you know, when Victor sets its cap to capture a percentage of any market, it usually gets what it is after, and then some."

An allied activity of real potential goes under the name Victor Educational Services Institute and was formally established in 1964.

Prior to the establishment of the educational department, the corporation sold machines to schools in about the same way it sold to any account, that is, to the school administrative offices. It takes many figuring machines to help with the payrolls, the billings, the invoices. But that is not where the big market is. The big market in education is the classroom where training is given in the use of machines. As a first step toward serving this market, Victor did extensive research to develop training courses for the schools, developing a graduated curriculum textbook. It starts off with a basic familiarization course and moves on up through calculating and the types of arithmetic problems encountered in business and the standard business forms used by corporations and, of course, high speed proficiency on the machines. "We are very pleased that our training material has won wide acceptance by educators. We have many testimonial letters to the effect that it is the finest material available on these subjects," stated sales manager Theo L. Fox, adding:

"Then, we have also set up a free training program for teachers, a 20-hour course on the use of Victor machines and the Victor educational material. In the first 18 months of the teacher program, more than 7,000 teachers in 137 cities went through the course and more programs are under way today than there were in the past.

"Another part of our activity is the training of people who are already on the job using figuring machines. You know, a top-of-the-line calculator costs around $635. Now it is going to cost an employer around $60,000 to have that machine operated by a person over the economic life of the machine, say ten years. So the real cost of the machine is $60,635.

"We've proved this right here with our own Victor office force. A simple, 11-hour training course using our textbook can increase adding speed 115 percent, increase ability in applying business machines to business arithmetic by 33 percent, and decrease human error. You apply these percentages to the $60,635 cost and you've got something that an employer can appreciate.

"As far as I know, Victor is the only company in the industry that provides software—textbooks and training programs—along with selling the hardware."

As for Victor's general outlook in machines, Fox says: "Now you know there were those who thought the advent of the computer meant the end of the desk-top adding-calculating machine. The year 1952 can be established as the year the computer made its first sizable inroads into American business. Since 1952, Victor's sales of desk-top adding and calculating machines have multiplied five times over. Part of the reason is the computer itself—its insatiable appetite for figures. The figures have to be worked with both on the input and the output sides of the computer.

"There is another very interesting thing going on. In that same year of 1952, the sale of typewriters to business offices exceeded the sale of adding-calculating machines by two to one. But in 1966, the sales of figuring machines exceeded typewriter sales. We have conducted surveys of our own all over the country and we find that there are more figuring machines than typewriters in actual use in offices today. And just recently the U. S. Labor Department forecast that by 1975 the country would need an increase of 106 percent in the number of figuring machine operators while an increase of only 26 percent would be needed in the number of people trained to use typewriters and to take shorthand and so forth.

"So, looking at all these things, new sales, the machines in use, and the forecast for the kinds of office workers needed, you see an imbalance between the needs of business and what the schools are doing. Our schools are still dealing with yesterday's problems. Counting the number of machines in use for training in the schools and the number of training hours, the emphasis is still nearly ten to one in favor of the typewriter. This is starting to change and we're taking every opportunity to suggest to the schools that they check with local business and find out the real needs.

"Education is generally recognized today as the nation's largest industry. There is no larger market. The company that has the equipment, the hardware and the software and the people to compete in this market is fortunate.

"Victor can compete."

In another area of growth potential, Victor is steadily building its position. Victor's Business Forms Group with a major headquarters plant at Lincoln, Nebraska, specialized plants at Merced, California; Arlington, Texas; Kalamazoo, Michigan; Nashville, Tennessee; and Atlanta, Georgia; and a high speed distribution center in New Jersey; is in an industry which will become a billion dollar industry in 1968.

"We have the basic elements," Forms Group President Harold R. Salisbury says, explaining:

"We're now one of the seven leading companies in the field. But there's a long gap between the big three of the industry—Moore, Standard, and UARCO—and the rest of us. There certainly is room and need for a strong number-four business forms company. We'll get to be number four and then worry about three and two.

"The big volume is in continuous and unit carbon sets—which Victor calls 'Kopy-Flo' and 'Ready-Rite'—used in computer and data processing systems. While I was president of the Business Forms Section of the Printing Industries of America, Inc. in 1967, our association undertook an in-depth market study and our conclusions show that the industry should have an 11 percent compound growth rate for the next five years. With 1967 sales of over $900 million, this would put the industry at $1.5 billion by 1972. That's the conservative forecast. If you want to be really optimistic and tie the business forms industry directly in with the number of computers that will be sold between now and then, you can get into much higher figures. The association's projection is on the conservative side because we realize that the computers to some degree are going to be using print-out or output methods other than paper. Therefore we used the 11 percent growth figure. Victor plans to get its share of this growth market."

A onetime footballer at the University of Nebraska, Salisbury has spent his business career with a predecessor company of the present Victor group. This was the Nebraska Salesbook Company, and Salisbury was general manager when the firm was acquired by

Comptometer. Salisbury comments:

"It was under Victor that we acquired some of the other key companies and for the first time put it all together under one head. Prior to that time, we had had separate manufacturing and separate sales organizations for each acquired company.

"It was an interesting transition from Comptometer to Victor, and I found out that management does make the difference. Mr. A. C. Buehler, Mr. Buehler, Jr., and Mr. Bakewell are vitally interested in our group and have materially assisted us in the formulation of our general objectives, and when we have problems they are more than happy to spend time with us helping solve these problems. But they don't tell us how to run the Forms Group. This is our responsibility and they hold us accountable for it.

"Victor has been putting far more money into the Forms Group than we can justify from our group's operation because management recognizes that we have needed money to build for the future. We have new buildings at Lincoln, Nebraska; Merced, California; and at Kalamazoo, Michigan. This is to say nothing of all the new, modern equipment we now have. The corporation has been willing to spend the money so that we can really take off into the future.

"Yes," Salisbury reemphasizes, "we have the basic elements and we are ready to go."

Once, in the 1920s, Victor had owned briefly a small company that manufactured pleasure boats. Then, twenty years later, there was the venture into the manufacture of golf carts. Always, A.C. had been an avid sportsman; despite his small stature, he had played a spirited game of football. And he had been a softball pitcher and a driver of racing boats. To say nothing of playing low-handicap golf.

Thus, both as a sportsman and as a businessman, A.C. was enthusiastic about the golf divisions acquired in the Comptometer merger. "This," A.C. says, "is a leisure-time business and most

Nebraska Sales Book Company
(top), founded in 1889,
provided foundation for present
Victor Business Forms Group.
Harold R. Salisbury (center),
Group president, inspects latest
type of chemical etching
equipment for making dry
offset plates at Kalamazoo,
Michigan forms plant.
"Kopy-Flo" continuous carbon
interleaved forms (left) are used
in data processing print-out.

people have more and more leisure time. Many holidays now provide three-day weekends and some day there may be a shorter work
week. And among leisure-time activities, golf is increasingly popular. Not long ago I saw that there were 651 golf courses under
construction in this country at one time. And now they are developing residential sections by starting out with a golf course and
selling the lots around it. It is no longer a game for the wealthy
only. You go back 15 years at Victor and I don't think we'd have
tried to run a company golf tournament. But now we have a couple
of hundred people turning out. I was out in a little town in Illinois
not long ago and they had a nice golf course. The club house
wasn't much, just an old house that happened to be there when
they built the course. But it was an 18-hole course and people
were playing. And those people use the same clubs and balls and
bags as they do at a club where there's a million dollar club house."

Victor's golf equipment operations are managed by President
Mark H. Cox, an experienced graduate of Wilson and Brunswick.
Ranking among the top companies in the field, Victor is again in
an excellent position to build sales. It is one of the few companies
in golfing equipment, according to Cox, that manufactures and
markets each of the three essentials for the golfer—clubs, bags and
balls. The three items account for the greater part of a market that
now produces more than $170 million a year in sales (at manu-
facturers' cost).

It was only a $30 million market in 1947; understandably golf
had taken a beating during the lean years of the Great Depression
and of World War II. Less than 5,000 courses were still in operation in 1946 and 1947. By the end of 1967 the number had jumped
to 8,337, to say nothing of nearly 900 par-3 courses and more than
4,500 driving ranges. Some 10 million golfers were playing about
180,000,000 rounds of golf a year.

Very quickly after the Comptometer merger, Victor management pulled the various golf companies into a single organization

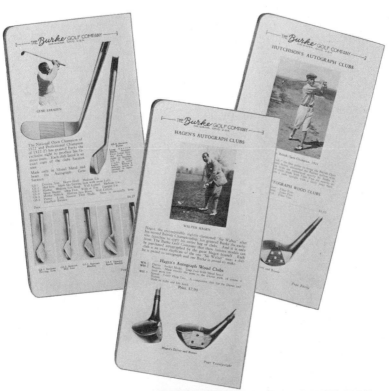

Shown above are pages from 1925 catalog of The Burke Golf Company, now a part of Victor's Burke-Worthington Division. Today's Burke-Worthington dealer line features clubs designed by Tommy Armour, golf's legendary Silver Scot. Pictured at right is Armour (seated) with Mark H. Cox, president of the Victor Golf Equipment Group.

and allocated new money for badly-needed modernization.

A new golf ball plant was built at Elyria, Ohio to replace an ancient and inefficient multistory layout. Much of the new machinery was designed by Worthington's long-time president, the late Robert F. Smith. The old plant was turning out something less than 900,000 dozen balls annually. The new plant has an ultimate annual capacity of 2,000,000 dozen. The former Burke Golf Equipment Corporation, founded in 1910 and the oldest exclusive maker of golf clubs in the U.S., now operates out of modern plants in Newark, Ohio and Morton Grove, Illinois. The newly-equipped Des Moines, Iowa plant makes golf bags, carryalls, head covers and accessories, including some under the famous Tufhorse name.

The Burke-Worthington division of Victor's Golf Equipment Group sells clubs, balls, bags and softwear through a growing number of dealers and retailers. Equipment of the PGA division, endorsed and approved by the Professional Golfers' Association of America and similarly endorsed by the CPGA in Canada, is sold exclusively by golf professionals.

Cox sizes up Victor's outlook on the golf course in these words:

"We have a very fine relationship with the Professional Golfers' Association of America, under which we have exclusive rights to market a broad line of golf equipment under the official PGA label.

"Another large share of the market is reached through sporting goods stores and the sporting goods sections of department, chain, discount, and other such stores.

"In an effort to increase our penetration of both these markets, we have reorganized and expanded our golf operations.

"We believe we are on the right track to greatly expand our activities in this field."

Total sales of the golf industry, Cox says, are increasing by about eight percent a year. And golf is only one of Victor's rather remarkable diversifications into the leisure-time market.

CHAPTER 13

"It's a Daisy!"

"The principal purpose of the acquisition of Daisy Manufacturing Company and its subsidiary, James Heddon's Sons, is to provide Victor with a more diversified line of products, particularly in the recreational field. The products to be added to Victor's business include air guns, play guns, BB shot and fishing equipment." This language was used in a letter to Victor Comptometer shareholders on April 21, 1967.

On another occasion, *Sports Illustrated*, in an article written by Joe David Brown, used more lyrical but just as accurate language to describe what it was that Victor was acquiring. Brown wrote: "Writers often recall with tender amusement the thrill of a boy's first kiss or his first pair of long pants. In the quiet part of the country where I grew up, most boys usually found one of these things disappointing and the other embarrassing. A real, memorable, intoxicating thrill of boyhood was aiming a Daisy for the first time and actually hitting something."

The Daisy air rifle has been a part of American boyhood almost from the day in 1886 when Lewis Cass Hough, vice president, general manager and part owner of the Plymouth Iron Windmill Co. of Plymouth, Michigan, examined a new product invented by the plant superintendent, Clarence J. Hamilton, and exclaimed: "Clarence, it's a daisy!"

For rather obvious reasons the windmill company, although it had been organized only a few years previously (1882), was looking for diversification. Hamilton's BB gun was right on target. Soon the company was producing nearly 300 guns a day and selling all it could produce at a wholesale price of 50 cents each. It did a $43,000 business in 1895 and Hough, Hamilton and company took progressively less interest in trying to sell iron windmills to the Michigan farmers.

By 1895, the name was the Daisy Manufacturing Company and kids all around the country were beginning to plink away at bottles and fence posts with Daisy rifles. The ancient Greeks had experimented with air-powered weapons, and an effective Austrian air gun was an issue in the Napoleonic wars—Bonaparte thought the air gun was unfair and he decreed that an Austrian captured with an air gun in his possession would be summarily shot. But it wasn't until the Hough family got Daisy well organized that the relatively harmless air gun became a well-known part of the everyday scene.

At 1967 annual meeting Daisy
Manufacturing Company and its subsidiary James
Heddon's Sons became part of Victor
Comptometer Corporation. Shown with
A. C. Buehler (center), Victor chairman,
are Cass S. Hough (left), former president
of Daisy and now president of the Victor
Daisy/Heddon Group, and Alvin F.
Bakewell, Victor president.

From the very beginning the Daisy BB rifle has been a pleasure or target gun with a carefully controlled muzzle velocity and an effective range of about 25 feet. The point was proven emphatically by the company's early-day supersalesman, Charles Bennett, a Hough cousin. Not long after the turn of the century when Charles Bennett succeeded Lewis Cass Hough as head of the company, and Edward C. Hough, son of Lewis, became secretary and treasurer, Daisy was doing a major export business as well.

The potentially big Chinese market remained closed to Daisy. Provincial warlords refused to issue import permits for any gun because they didn't want anyone but their own soldiers to possess the means of doing battle. To them, the Daisy was a gun. To salesman Bennett this was the supreme challenge. Traveling to China, he succeeded in getting an audience with the key warlord and was rapidly losing the sales battle when he had an inspiration. Striding a few feet away, he turned around, bent over and invited the warlord to fire away. Gleefully, the Chinese complied. Uncle Charlie, as he was known in the company, confessed later that, wearing skin-tight trousers as he was, he never had anything hurt so much in all his life. But he came up smiling and the warlord promptly put his stamp on the import license. This was in 1907 and China provided a good Daisy market right up to World War II; for years it was among the top three Daisy markets overseas.

A few years later, in 1912, another man made a large contribution to Daisy. His name was Charles F. LeFever, an accomplished St. Louis gunsmith. LeFever had invented a new type of air rifle, and Daisy was to manufacture it. LeFever came to Plymouth for six weeks to show the Daisy production people how to make the gun. As matters turned out, the six weeks stretched into 43 years, until his death in 1961 at age 93. Like Victor, Daisy has always been a high-quality manufacturer and it was LeFever, the master gunmaker, who did much to establish that quality. But the contribution he's known for was the 1913 invention, a pump action BB gun, the first pump model ever made and until a few years ago, the most famous of the Daisy line of guns. With a few modifications it is still in the Daisy catalog along with the lever action guns and the modern variations of both.

Charles H. Bennett and Edward C. Hough ran Daisy for almost six decades until succeeded by Edward's son, Cass S. Hough, in 1959. Born in 1904, Cass S. Hough, still trim and athletic today, is the holder of Michigan pilot registration number one, a qualified jet pilot, a sports car buff and a collector of 18th century French furniture. He started out to be an astronomer and taught astronomy for one year at the University of Michigan after graduating in 1925 with honors. But he soon deserted the campus for business and quickly proved his mettle as a merchandiser.

By the late 1920s, Daisy was clearly the dominant company in its field, having outsold the competition or having acquired competing companies. The King company had been bought by Edward Cass Hough and Charles H. Bennett personally just before the first World War and it was operated as a separate company until 1931 when it was finally merged into Daisy. In 1927 King needed a new operating head so Bennett and the elder Hough dispatched young Cass to King headquarters with some heavy-handed kidding—his orders were to run Daisy out of business. Cass was doing a remarkably good job of accomplishing just that when the bottom dropped out with the advent of the Great Depression. In 1931, the King machinery was moved into the Daisy plant and the operations were consolidated. To this day, Cass Hough retains the sneaking suspicion that his father and Bennett used the depression as an excuse to get rid of King before Cass became too much of an embarrassment.

Cass has carried on the traditions of Daisy manufacturing—he once junked several thousand rifles because of a defect in the rifle

Plymouth Iron Wind Mill Co. in 1889, forerunner of Daisy Manufacturing Company The Daisy dray, in 1909, loaded with sacks of BB guns ready for shipment. Illustrations below track the history of air rifles—(1) bellows-type, 1820, (2) Daisy's all metal construction with skeleton stock, 1889, (3) Daisy's CO_2 300 semi-automatic gas-operated BB rifle, and (4) the revolutionary new Daisy V/L .22 rifle featuring caseless ammunition and air ignition system. Its distinguishing cocking lever is shown in open position.

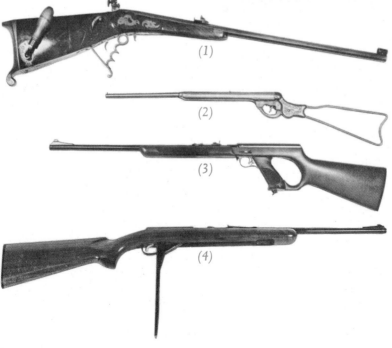

(1)

(2)

(3)

(4)

forearm that was not visible to the layman's eye—but he's been a constant and effective innovator, too. In products and merchandising and in other ways. Early in his career he started arranging tie-ins which would identify Daisy with popular heroes peopling the minds of his young customers. He introduced, for instance, such best sellers as the Buck Jones, Buzz Barton and Red Ryder lines of air rifles. Cass himself tells about one coup:

"Dick Calkins, who was drawing Buck Rogers, had a gun of sorts in Buck's hand. I went to see John Dille, the head of the National Newspaper Syndicate selling Buck Rogers, in Chicago and I told him that if Daisy could design a rocket gun and Calkins would put it in the strip, we could both make some money. We'd make a profit on the sales, and the syndicate and Calkins would get a royalty. We agreed to do it and Daisy went to work on the Buck Rogers rocket pistol. I wrote a lot of the nomenclature and a lot of continuity that was used in the strip. Calkins started feeding the nomenclature into the strip about six months before the pistol was put on the market.

"It became one of the best selling toys of all time. The Macy's-Gimbels story is amusing. Macy's had been given an exclusive on the rocket pistol for the first week it came out. Gimbels, of course, didn't like this. The minute Macy's started off offering the pistol at 49 cents, Gimbels sent shoppers over there to buy as many as they could. Then, Gimbels put them on sale at 47 cents. Soon they were in a real price war and both stores were selling them as fast as they could put them on the counter. I was in New York and soon we ran out of pistols to sell to Macy's. So I hired a bunch of girls to go into both Macy's and Gimbels and buy as many as they could. I set up headquarters in the old McAlpin Hotel across the street from the stores and we'd re-box the pistols and take them around to the delivery entrance at Macy's and sell them again. They were screaming for more pistols. These plus what we were making at the factory kept them happy and it was good business for us. Early in the price war that was going on, they got the retail price down below our wholesale price, so we were buying the pistols for less than they cost us to make at the factory. This went on for three or four days, until the end of the Macy's exclusive. Eventually, both stores found out the whole story and we all had a good laugh."

There's an appropriate footnote to the story. Of course, the famous Buck Rogers rocket pistol disappeared from the scene along with other non-essential goods during World War II. But Hough saved the tools and after the war brought the rocket pistol out again, this time as the atomic pistol. Again, Daisy was swamped with orders.

At the time Cass Hough became president, the company, seeking expansion room and escape from an accumulation of outmoded machinery and buildings and a poor economic climate, moved from Michigan to Rogers, Arkansas in the Ozark hunting and fishing country. There Hough built a 3,200-square-foot-apartment onto the new Daisy office building so that he could keep right on top of things, and he kept a twin-engine plane at the Rogers airport so he could get quickly to Daisy's other installations, customers and sales offices.

Today Daisy makes and markets 264 products and models ranging from a precision-made $170 retail match-target pellet rifle through standard BB guns, CO_2 BB rifles and pistols and toy guns that do such things as make ricochet noises, produce smoke, fire corks and knock down targets with an authentic shock wave. BB air guns and BBs account for a little less than half of the Daisy sales. The plants turn out an amazing 1,500,000 BB guns a year, another 3,000,000 guns and pistols of other kinds and more than 54,000,000 BBs each day.

The annually-increasing demand for Daisy guns and ammunition has been stimulated by long years of Daisy pioneering in the promotion of correct shooting programs for youths. The emphasis belongs on the word "correct." With Daisy help, millions of boys and girls in the Boy Scouts, 4-H Clubs, Boys Clubs and school and summer camp programs have learned to handle guns properly and with respect. In 1967 alone, more than 1,000,000 youngsters, 7 to 14 years old, received supervised training in shooting programs through the U.S. Jaycees-Daisy Shooting Education Project. The Jaycees top off the annual program with the International BB gun matches which, in 1968, drew champion shooters from 39 states, Canada, and Mexico.

But the fun of BB gun shooting is not for youngsters only. Daisy can count among its many fans more and more adults who are discovering the recreational value of this type of shooting. Gun clubs are now instituting air gun programs and state conservation departments are utilizing BB guns for hunter training programs.

Another factor in Daisy's growth is the Daisy promotion of at-home, indoor shooting. The low velocity and short range of the Daisy BB guns makes possible safe, low cost, quiet shooting in the basement or recreation room. This indoor shooting is proving to be a popular family participation sport.

Daisy's unbelievable total of 54,000,000 BBs a day doesn't include several million BBs now being produced daily for the U.S. Armed Forces and for a program that represents a major innovation in the training of American infantrymen. Daisy air guns, modified to more nearly approximate standard infantry rifles, are used to give soldiers training of the type never before possible. BB guns, accurate at short range, can be used for familiarization and target practice at a cost far less than if the standard rifle and ammunition were used. Then, too, the trainee, wearing protective goggles, can be given realistic field training in the kind of warfare encountered by American soldiers in Korea and Viet Nam—quick aiming and firing under surprise conditions.

Early ads for Daisy air rifles include one used in China. Shown below are the finals of annual International BB Gun Matches, co-sponsored by Daisy and the U.S. Jaycees. Through this program, more than 1,000,000 youngsters annually receive training in fundamentals of safety and marksmanship.

The Daisy BB air rifle has become important to the U.S. Army and allied forces in the "Quick Kill" combat training. This "no aim" shooting method is based on the sport shooter's principle that when a person points his finger at something, the object, his finger and his eye fall into perfect alignment. It happens instinctively. The Daisy rifle offers an economical and safe way to teach this method of shooting. During 1968, more than 90,000 Daisy training rifles were in use in this program.

Daisy was also selected by the Air Force as a prime supplier of special cold-headed ball products.

Daisy, of course, cooperates with the Pentagon, but military work is not the company's forte. Referring to the company's research and development program, Hough commented in 1967: "At the request of the United States Army, much R & D time at Daisy was devoted to developing material to be used in the training of recruits. This development included everything from BB gun sighting systems to the use of BB guns in simulated ground-to-air training. Some of the devices designed and built and given to the Army to evaluate cannot be revealed, but suffice it to say that these demands on our already overloaded R & D department seriously delayed the completion of consumer goods projects, many of which were to have been completed for the 1966 and early 1967 marketing seasons."

One of those delayed projects—delayed by R & D requirements and by Viet Nam war priorities imposed on Daisy suppliers—could turn out to be one of the biggest developments in Daisy's history and in the history of sport shooting.

The story goes back to 1961—and to Paris. Cass S. Hough was in Europe, checking on Daisy sales and looking around for new ideas. A friend suggested a chat with a Belgian petrochemist-engineer named Jules E. Van Langenhoven. For some years, Van Langenhoven had been experimenting with new ways to fire a bullet from a gun. Specifically, he had been trying to find a way to reduce the weight and the cost of the cartridge. Both the cost and the weight of a conventional bullet are primarily in the brass case, the cap and the primer charge in the cap. Question: how to eliminate the case, cap and primer? Inventors and gunsmiths have been working on the answer to the question almost from the very day that the modern cartridge system was developed—stuffing the rifle with powder, wadding and ball and igniting the powder by one means or another. Actually, in the years just prior to the American Civil War, two later-to-be-famous mechanics named Smith and Wesson thought they had the answer. But the propellants they attached to the rear of the lead slug failed to give the bullet enough oomph and quickly corroded the inside of the barrel.

Hough found out Van Langenhoven's answer when he met the chemist by arrangement at a rifle range off the Champs Elysees in May of 1961. Van Langenhoven was full of technical information; he had been working with a nitrocellulose derivative. But it was the simple, straightforward demonstration given by the inventor that impressed Hough. The firing range was equipped with instrumentation for clocking bullet speed.

Van Langenhoven showed Hough a rifle that Hough recognized as a popular German-made air gun which fired a pellet. The chemist had made his own modifications of the air mechanism.

Van Langenhoven loaded the gun and fired. The chronograph flashed the speed of the pellet: 350 feet per second, slightly above the short-range speed of a Daisy BB. The Belgian took a small tin out of his pocket and opened it, revealing a substance that looked like dirty gray cotton. Van Langenhoven pinched off a small bit of the stuff and pressed it into a space hollowed out in a pellet. Loading up, he fired again. The chronograph flashed: 700 feet per second. Van Langenhoven pinched off a larger bit of the cotton-like material, loaded and fired. Speed: 1,000-plus feet per second, approaching the speed of a conventional .22 caliber bullet.

That did it right there for Cass S. Hough. After a short discussion, Hough and Van Langenhoven shook hands on a development deal and Hough sealed the bargain by scribbling out a personal check and handing it to the Belgian. He had already made up his mind that if the Daisy board of directors didn't share his enthusiasm he'd personally undertake the commercial development of the idea.

There was no trouble from that source. But, obviously, there was much work to be done: the rifle mechanism had to be perfected and put into a rifle that could be produced and marketed at an attractive price; the secret propellant would have to be tested under all conditions for such things as stability and firepower, and a caseless bullet would have to be designed and standardized.

At first, technicians hired by Daisy worked in a lab set up in an old nursery office building on the north end of the property Daisy bought in Rogers, Arkansas. Van Langenhoven came to this country to work full time on the project, now code named Project V/L for the inventor. At the same time, Hough hired researchers at Chicago's famous Illinois Institute of Technology to rerun the Daisy experiments and double check the results.

Compared with the Van Langenhoven concept, the conventional shooting system is a Rube Goldberg contraption with its trigger, cocking mechanism, hammer, primer charge, explosive powder, projectile, and the mechanism for extracting and ejecting the spent case. The V/L rifle as finally developed by Daisy is comparatively simple: The trigger releases a plunger in an air chamber, the plunger drives forward and compresses the air in the chamber. When air is compressed rapidly it has a fast temperature rise. In the Daisy rifle this hot compressed air shoots through a valve and into the firing chamber at temperatures around 2,000 degrees. This immediately ignites the propellant loaded into the base of the Daisy bullet. In the manner of an Apollo space missile, the bullet pushes off and picks up speed as the propellant burns and the lead slug moves down the barrel.

The simplicity of the V/L mechanism introduces a new era of sports shooting. The V/L caseless ammunition eliminates the cartridge and primer. There is no need for a complicated extraction and ejection mechanism which limits the speed of automatic guns and often causes jamming. And, the V/L system has no residue and practically eliminates gun cleaning. In actual tests, V/L guns have been shot 50,000 times before minimal cleaning was required. Since V/L ammo has no case and the propellant is completely consumed on firing, there is nothing left to foul the gun barrel.

Cass S. Hough comments: "This new V/L era means low cost shooting whether you are shooting trap, skeet, or target or plinking. V/L caseless ammo costs less because of the elimination of the case and primer, traditionally the most expensive parts of a conventional bullet. The V/L requires little molding, another expense. A round of V/L weighs only about 60 percent of the weight of a conventional round, another cost reduction factor, all tending to keep V/L shooting costs at a minimum.

"Our propellant and the shooting system are equally applicable to other kinds of guns, to all types of shooting. We're starting out with a single shot .22 caliber rifle which is now in production. Then, we'll have a .22 repeater and we hope soon after that to have a semi-automatic. We can take some of the high pressure gas generated by the burning of the propellant and use its pressure to reset the action for the next shot, just as is done in an ordinary semi-automatic rifle of the conventional type. Laboratory studies indicate a fine application for the V/L principle in the ordinary shotgun—an application that would again eliminate the big hunk of brass and the primer. And we've been able to marry a bunch of bird shot to a piece of our propellant.

"Theoretically, we could sell a V/L gun to every shooter in the country. We have done some market studies and I just put the figures in my drawer. Literally, they scare me. I don't think they could be accurate.

"We know this has military applications and the military does, too. We just haven't had the time or the people to work on it. A G.I. could carry more rounds for the same weight or the same number of rounds at a lower weight. And, of course, it could have similar weight advantages for airborne troops and for aircraft. Then, the rate of fire of an automatic weapon is basically determined by the length of time it takes for the mechanism to reach in and extract and eject the empty case. When you don't have a case to extract, or a mechanism to jam, you can dramatically increase the rate of fire of an automatic weapon. There also seems to be unlimited use of the propellant in other fields."

Among other diversifications, the company has its Daisy/Heddon Limited plant at Preston, Ontario, where a selected Daisy line is manufactured and the Blazon line of playground equipment is manufactured for sale in Canada under license from Blazon, Inc., the U. S. manufacturer.

Daisy accomplished its major diversification when it acquired James Heddon's Sons, one of the most widely-known makers of fishing tackle with a history going back before the turn of the century.

James Heddon, the founder of the company, was a recognized authority on bees who began his business career as a manufacturer of beekeeping equipment in Dowagiac, Michigan. In 1889, while fishing at the local millpond, he flipped a whittled stick into the water and was amazed to see a big bass strike the stick.

The incident gave Heddon the idea for a wooden fishing lure. By 1892, he had perfected a fishing plug which met with instant acceptance in his community.

James Heddon, founder of
James Heddon's Sons and
creator of one of the best known
lines of fishing tackle; his
original wood-carved lure (top)
and a modern version of the
same lure; center is early
Heddon delivery truck.
Heddon's new line of salt-water
tackle (below) features the
Dominator ocean trolling reel.

Soon, Heddon was marketing his lure widely, using his bee-keeping equipment dealers as outlets. By 1897, Heddon realized there was more honey in fishing tackle than in bees and he turned to tackle manufacturing exclusively.

From his modest start, Heddon became the top-line manufacturer in the field and a great innovator. He was the first to produce the forerunner of the present casting rod designs. He designed and patented the first offset rod handle with screw-locking reel seat, still the best rod handle design on the market. He patented the most widely known lure of all times, the River Runt, the first plastic spook or transparent lure. Other famous Heddon classical lures followed: Lucky 13, Crazy Crawler, Chugger, the Sonic, to name just a few, all recognized as among the greatest fish catchers in the industry.

Company projections indicate a bright future for this addition to Victor's position in the leisure-time market. Heddon is as well known among fishermen as Daisy is in its field. And its market is growing more than 10 percent a year. Known for its higher priced and quality tackle, Heddon has introduced a low and medium priced line of fresh water reels and rods, as well as a line of salt water equipment. These innovations should mean that Heddon will move on from its traditional niche at the top of the line to become a major factor in the production and sale of fishing tackle in all fields and in all price ranges.

In all, when the merger between Victor and Daisy (and the D & H Corporation, an investment company of the famed Murchison family of Texas, which owned 53 percent of the Daisy stock as its principal asset) became effective on May 18, 1967, Victor had acquired $19,100,000 in gross sales and $1,190,000 in earnings. These were the Daisy figures for the calendar and fiscal year 1966.

CHAPTER 14

Business with Pleasure

December, 1967, was a good month for Victor. And for two men named Fred. On December 8, A.C. and Fred F. Ertl, Jr., announced that The Ertl Company, Dyersville, Iowa manufacturer of "live action scale models of farm equipment," was joining the Victor family of recreational product companies. On December 13, A.C. and Fred Bear announced that Bear Archery Company, Grayling, Michigan, maker of the best in target and hunting bows, arrows and accessories, was also joining Victor.

The two companies together added about $10 million in annual sales to the Victor total. Both were generating profits at a healthy rate and both held the possibility of strong expansion, especially with the support that Victor could offer.

And both companies are in the best tradition of American entrepreneurship: they were founded and built by men with little else than an idea and determination. In the lives of both founders, accident and adversity played a major role.

One of the crucial years for Fred Bear was 1927. At the time, he was a patternmaker and a technical consulting engineer for the Packard Motor Car Company in Detroit. Fortunately for him, he happened to see a movie called *Alaskan Adventure*, featuring the bow and arrow accomplishments of Art Young, a widely-known sportsman and the first modern-day archer to claim an Alaskan Kodiak bear as a trophy. Immediately, Fred had a new hobby. He bought a lemonwood stave and other necessary materials, made his own bow and arrow set, and taught himself to shoot.

By 1933, he had become skilled enough to give shooting demonstrations at sports shows and for other groups. By this time he was superintendent of Jansen Manufacturing Company, a manufacturer of golf equipment.

At this point, accident intervened significantly—the factory burned and Bear's job disappeared in the flames.

Instead of joining the swelling army of the unemployed in that Great Depression period, Bear decided to go in business for himself. The ingredients of the business were a few hundred dollars in savings, some woodworking equipment, and Fred's consuming interest in archery. If starting a new business in 1933 was a high-risk venture, starting one in the recreation-hobby field probably ranked in the near-impossible category. Especially so when Bear's intent is examined. He was not out to sell the cowboys and Indians toy market; he meant to make bows and arrows for the serious

Fred Bear (above left), founder of Bear Archery,
was second man to officially claim an Alaskan Kodiak bear
with bow and arrow. Quality equipment has attracted
ladies and children into fast-growing sport of archery
target shooting. Bear Archery Museum (below),
which contains archery trophies and artifacts from
all parts of the world, is located at Grayling, Michigan,
known as the "Archery Capital of the World."

archer, not exactly a plentiful creature, and the bowhunter, a type almost extinct after the real Indians adopted the white man's gun.

The first bows Bear made sold in a price range not inexpensive in those unaffluent times—$21.50 to $49.50. There were weeks when it seemed that the young company couldn't go on. But Bear did gradually create and build his market. First, he helped found and promote the Detroit Archery Club (still going strong today, the club had an original membership of eight). Then he spent what time he could doing what he loved to do; hunting with bow and arrow. And he made certain that the newspapers were supplied with pictures of the bowhunter with his game. A man with an appreciation of nature and of the drama of the hunter, armed only with bow and arrow, stalking large and small game, and a man with a flair for words, Bear became the subject of many a newspaper and magazine interview. And wrote many an article himself.

The fact that the sport of bowhunting has achieved the status and recognition it now enjoys among legislators, conservationists, members of the press and sportsmen is due in no small part to Bear's personal efforts and expenditures. His many appearances before state commissions and committees strongly influenced 1937 legislation under which Michigan became one of the first states in the Union to establish a separate bowhunting season. That first season, fewer than 200 licenses were sold. Today, Michigan has more than 50,000 bowhunters in the field annually.

Bear has been all over the world (he became the second man to officially claim an Alaskan Kodiak bear with the bow), hunting, taking pictures, making movie films and writing. He is often referred to as the man who did more for archery than anyone since Robin Hood.

Archery is big sport and a big business today. Annual retail sales nationally are booming into the $50 million area. More than eight

million Americans are active in the sport, every state now having
a bowhunting season.

There are more than 5,000 archery clubs and indoor ranges
around the country and Bear estimates that the number of licensed
bowhunters is over a million.

Bear Archery employs more than 300 persons at its plant in
Grayling, deep in the upper Michigan hunting country, where the
company has been located since 1947. It turns out as many as
70,000 laminated wood and fiber glass bows a year with prices
ranging up to $175. About 25 percent are tournament bows. It
manufactures more than two million arrows annually and also
makes related equipment, e.g., quivers, armguards, and shooting
gloves. It also distributes a line of camouflage clothing for the
hunter and the backpacking and camping equipment made by
Himalayan Industries.

Operating as a division of Victor, Bear Archery expects to
broaden its lines and expand its sales at an even faster rate. As Fred
Bear says, "All of us here at Bear are happy about our association
with Victor and look forward eagerly to an exciting future."

It was in the summer of 1945 that accident intervened in the
life of Fred F. Ertl, Sr. A German-born immigrant, he was living
in Dubuque, Iowa with his wife and five sons. He was a metal
molder by trade and good at his job. Except that he had no job
that summer. The factory where he worked had been closed tight
in what turned out to be a long and bitter strike. With some
thought of making a little extra money, Ertl retired to the basement of the family home and filled the idle days making toys—
miniature tractors, cars, and airplanes—molded from aluminum.
In the family car, loaded up with his toys, Ertl would drive from
store to store in the area selling his models. When the supply was
exhausted, he would rush home to make more.

In 1946, craftsman and tinkerer Ertl was a businessman. He had a contract with Deere & Co. to produce toy models of the John Deere line of tractors and farm equipment. They were exact scale models and they were sold through the regular Deere farm equipment dealers.

Ertl had hit upon a likely combination: the models were not only attractive toys, but they also had real promotional value for Deere & Co. and its dealers. Today the Ertl Company is a tiny giant, the largest toy farm equipment manufacturer in the world, turning out as many as 20,000 units a day—tractors, trucks, trailers, plows, hay rakes, bulldozers. The toys that pour off the five production lines at the company's 150,000 square-foot plant in Dyersville, Iowa are exact scale die-cast aluminum models of the real thing, down to the paint job and the name of the manufacturer.

The names are important. Ertl has exclusive contracts with the major companies in the farm equipment industry: Deere & Co., International Harvester, Allis-Chalmers, Oliver, J. I. Case, Le-Tourneau-Westinghouse, Caterpillar, Minneapolis-Moline, Ford, Massey-Ferguson, New Holland and White Motors. The only toy company authorized to use the names and trademarks, Ertl has close and confidential working relationships with the equipment manufacturers that enable the firm to keep up to date on design changes and new models.

The Ertl plant chews up more than 2,000,000 pounds of aluminum and 750,000 pounds of zinc a year turning out the toys to satisfy an expanding market. Not only are the toys moved through the thousands of farm equipment dealers in the United States and Canada, but also through an increasing number of standard retail stores.

In addition to the scale-model toys, Ertl has a second profitable line—riding tractors, or "kid-size miniatures of king-size tractors," as the company catalog says. Again exact replicas of name brand

The Ertl Company produces a broad line of scale model toy trucks and tractors. Shown below are Mr. and Mrs. Fred Ertl and their five sons during early days when "family production" turned out 150 tractors on a good day. Today the Ertl plant in Dyersville, Iowa produces as many as 20,000 units in a day.

TRACTORS...

...HE BUILDS MORE THAN ANYONE The assembly line at Fred Ertl's tractor works can produce as many as 10,000 units per day, which makes him the world's largest tractor manufacturer. But, as you can see from the photo at left of Ertl with one of his production models, none of them are very big. His "tractors", see next page

tractors, the rubber-tired models are equipped with bicycle-type pedals and chain drive and come with or without a trailer.

The company also has a profitable industrial sideline. Using its expertise in die-casting, it produces a number of aluminum parts under contract to manufacturing firms.

By the time the Ertl Company joined the Victor family, Fred Ertl, Sr. had turned active management of the firm over to his five sons. Fred, Jr. was president. Looking back, he could recall that the company had come "a long way from the days when Dad would melt down aluminum airplane pistons in the furnace of our home . . . We had the warmest house in town. The windows would be wide open in the middle of winter. Mom was the paint department and my brothers and I put on the wheels after school. We could make 150 tractors on a good day."

Looking forward, he was sure that the company would go a long way in the future with the help of Victor management know-how and capital and its established channels of distribution. As Fred Ertl, Jr. says, "The only problem preventing rapid and large growth has been our lack of capital. The markets are there but available money was not. Our new association with Victor has solved the problem and there is every indication of greater progress to come in the very near future."

One of the men who had watched Victor's growth and who had participated in the day-to-day decisions was Albert C. Buehler, Jr., the executive vice president of the corporation and the president of the Business Machines Group.

A.C.'s son celebrated his 45th birthday the same year Victor celebrated its 50th anniversary. Bert Buehler had been at that time a Victor employee for 26 years and a member of management in progressively higher capacities for 20 years. Realistically and perceptively, he comments:

"Victor wouldn't be what it is today—or will be tomorrow—

if it weren't for Dad. This is our 50th anniversary and he has been here almost as long. In a way, he is Victor and Victor is Dad and it is hard to separate the two. Certainly, Victor never really took off until he was in full charge. I don't care what you call it, spirit, team spirit, or whatever, but he generated it and instilled it and it carries on down the line. I'm not worried about it lasting and I'm not worried about Victor. He's a very successful leader and what he has built has become deeply ingrained in everybody in the whole organization and it will continue.

"In many ways this is a unique place to work. I doubt if there are very many hundred-million dollar plus corporations in this country where a young man in the mail room could come in and discuss a problem with the chairman of the board. But if the problem didn't involve the man's superior, or something like that, there couldn't be a happier guy in the world than A.C. would be to counsel with him. I don't think there are very many people around here who don't feel that they have an absolutely open door to anyone they want to talk to, the chairman, the president, and on down the line.

"He is an amazing guy to sit back and look at. He can get pretty determined and be pretty sure he's right. In most cases, he has been. I can't say I was terribly in favor of the Comptometer acquisition. And Bake and some of the others weren't any more in favor of it than I was. But A.C. saw what there was in it. I would also say that once the decision was firm everyone around here worked as hard as he could work to make it go. That's the kind of organization we have.

"But, as I say, Dad can be pretty sure he's right and he can demand a lot of other people. But there's also a great flexibility to him. He'll allow you to run with the ball and make a mistake. However, he really isn't too fond of the same mistake again. I don't think he has ever said to a man, 'why were you dumb enough

to make that mistake?' He wouldn't do it that way. He's not in-
tolerant of errors. But I don't think anyone makes the same one
again. He gets more out of people that way than by beating them.
He's really a very soft person. I'm not sure he's ever really fired
anybody.

"For himself, my father has one way to go into things and that's
all the way. If he's going to do something in business, he's going
to concentrate on it and give it all he has. He'll take risks but they
are calculated risks and he works to make them turn out right.

"He's the same way with his hobbies, and he has many of them.
When he went into Lippizaner horses, he went in and bought—
I don't know how many; he must have had 20. I think he had more
Lippizaners than anybody except the Spanish Riding School in
Vienna. Certainly the most in this country. Then he decided to
switch to Shetlands and he has one of the very biggest—and best
—Shetland operations in the country. And he really runs that farm
of his.

"The farm is his hobby and his relaxation, but he runs it about
the way he runs his business. You know, the records are all there,
be it the breeding records or the feed records, and everything is
shipshape. This is the way my dad goes into everything; this is
relaxation for him, though.

"You might almost say Dad enjoys making a business out of a
hobby and solving the problems of the hobby. It's marvelous and
I admire him for it and I think maybe a little of it has rubbed off
on me. I hope so."

CHAPTER 15

It All Adds Up to Growth

On April 26, 1968, A. C. Buehler boarded a Pan American transatlantic jet at the Chicago International terminal. He was headed for Frankfurt and for Hannover, where the greatest of the European office equipment shows was in progress.

A.C. intended to pay a visit to the Victor display at the Hannover Fair, but he was even more interested in what might be going on at another booth, one carrying the Heinz Nixdorf company insigne. On the scene, A.C. was delighted to find that the Nixdorf display was one of the more popular in the entire fair.

Since January, Victor had become increasingly interested in the Nixdorf company. The operative word was "computer."

Sixteen years previously, Heinz Nixdorf, only 43 in 1968, had been a brilliant student of physics at the University of Frankfurt. At a time when the computer was still in its infancy and generally thought of as the multimillion-dollar experiment of giant corporations and government agencies, Nixdorf had become convinced that the amazing time and labor saving capabilities of computer technology could be made available to medium-size and small companies. If a small, relatively inexpensive electronic data processing unit could be designed to perform certain basic functions with computer efficiency, the unit could be sold at a price that would fit the pocketbook of the smaller company.

While still a student, Nixdorf and an assistant designed, assembled and sold such a computer. Building on that success, he was in 1968 the owner of a thriving firm with some 700 employees at its plant and research laboratories at Paderborn, near Dusseldorf. He had sold some 5,000 small computers specifically designed to handle payroll, accounting, billing and allied functions. Anticipating sales in excess of 4,000 units in 1968 alone, mostly in Germany, Nixdorf was thinking seriously of foreign markets.

To this end, his representative had been talking to a group in New York about setting up a marketing and service organization in the United States. Included in the group was a German national, a former Victor employee. In natural course, the German called at the New York Victor regional office to sound the company's interest. This was in January. After that, events moved swiftly.

Victor officers flew to New York to look at the Nixdorf computer. A machine was shipped to the Victor research center in Chicago where electronics experts and engineers went over it in detail. Marketing studies were instituted.

"We were impressed from the beginning with the quality of the workmanship," says a Victor executive with a long background in the computer industry, "and with the fact that the Nixdorf 820 was not a hybrid. Making use of the most advanced electronic and computer technology, it was designed as a small computer capable of performing a variety of functions with maximum efficiency. Competitive systems on the market are generally electro-mechanical machines to which electronics have been added. As such, they have the severe limitations inherent in a hybrid."

Following a full scale presentation by Victor technical and marketing people, the board of directors gave the go-ahead for serious explorations with Nixdorf. A series of transatlantic flights followed, involving A.C., Alvin Bakewell, Heinz Nixdorf and others.

On June 20, 1968, midway through its golden anniversary year, Victor announced that it had signed a marketing agreement with Nixdorf. Under a long-term contract, the Nixdorf computer systems would be sold by Victor, under the Victor name, in the United States and Canada.

The contract gave Victor, already the largest maker of figuring machines, a foothold in another vast market, the market for electronic accounting and billing machines. And put Victor in that market on the basis of the most advanced of technologies, computer science.

Actually, the new Victor computer systems opened up two, if not three, distinct and almost unlimited markets for the company. The machines, selling from $8,500 to $80,000, depending on capacity and the amount and sophistication of peripheral input-output equipment, are designed for the use of the thousands of smaller businesses which have no need for the huge, general purpose computers offered by the IBMs and Sperry Rands. But at $10,000 or $20,000, or $50,000, or on the basis of a lease, they can profit from putting payrolls, accounting, billing and inventory records on an efficient digital computer system.

A second great market is in the use of the machines as terminals. A bank, an airline, a major industrial corporation using a general purpose computer may need hundreds of terminals, both in the home office and the field to feed information into the main computer and to receive it—in compatible machine-talk. The Victor-Nixdorf machine could be installed, for instance, in the St. Louis branch sales office and warehouse of a New York headquartered manufacturing company. In St. Louis, the unit would take care of all bookkeeping needs in detail while providing New York with summary information needed for control and management information.

A third market might be labeled "all other." Nixdorf has already sold the machine to schools for programmed learning purposes and to industrial companies for process control and monitoring uses. It has been estimated that sales of small, specialized digital computers to the technical-industrial market are increasing even faster than the phenomenal growth rate shown by large general business computers.

The negotiations with Heinz Nixdorf produced an unexpected bonus for Victor. One week before A.C. flew to the Hannover Fair, Nixdorf signed an agreement of his own providing for the acquisition of Wanderer Werke, A.G., Cologne. Wanderer is an old-line, top-notch German manufacturer of business machines. Among its products was a line of advanced electronic printing calculators.

For several years General Micro-electronics, a subsidiary of Philco-Ford, had been working to develop for Victor one of these electronic marvels with their ability to calculate in milliseconds and their computer-related abilities in the area of limited memory and programming. The space-age technology that was the heart of the machine, however, had stubbornly resisted efforts to bend it to the demands of mass production. Accordingly, a favorable and

A. C. Buehler, Jr. (left), Victor director,
executive vice president and president of
Business Machines Group, holds program
panel as he and Vernon R. Loucks, director
and general counsel, view new Victor
electronic accounting and billing computer.

amicable settlement terminating Victor's contract for these machines was reached.

The Wanderer line was fully competitive with what was on the market and ahead of the market in some important respects. Very quickly Victor checked the machines and the production facilities and began negotiations to add the Wanderer calculators to the agenda for discussions with Nixdorf. The result was a second agreement. Victor would become the exclusive distributor of the desk-top electronic printing calculator under the Victor name, not only in the United States and Canada but also throughout the world.

With its strong existing sales force for adding machines and electro-mechanical calculators, and with the spadework and training accomplished for the General Micro-electronics machine, Victor was in an excellent position to capitalize on the Wanderer agreement.

Marketing the computer series was to be a more difficult proposition. A sales, service, and systems force had to be recruited and trained from scratch. While Nixdorf put into motion plans to increase the output of the Paderborn plant, Victor scheduled the opening of three initial branch offices for the computer marketing organization: New York, Los Angeles and Chicago. Plans called for the opening of other branch offices as the build-up progressed. These organizational costs obviously would preclude profits in 1968 and possibly 1969 from computer sales but the investment should eventually be worth the cost.

Nixdorf makes a variety of computer-related input and output and communications devices which also will be marketed by Victor. Some sources indicate that, in dollars, the market for this peripheral equipment and for terminals could exceed the market for general purpose computers, phenomenal as that is.

At age 50, Victor was not by any means resting on its oars. A.C. was able to say that at no time in the company's history were more new product development projects under way in the Business Machines Group. Bert Buehler, president of the group, reported on some of them. The electronics capability of the Victor research department was beefed up and the lab was given a new budget for the development of an electronic calculator that would display problems and answers on a cathode ray tube. While the Wanderer electronic printing calculator, or Victor Series 1500 as it was named, would print a permanent record on tape of problem and answer at the incredible speed of 60 characters a second, the cathode ray tube system would mean practically instantaneous display of the figures.

Also in the works was an adding machine design that would mean an improved machine at a better price in the low end of the Victor line. Then there was the Series 10 electro-mechanical calculator, a high-speed automatic printing calculator with grand total and short-cut multiplication capabilities, highly competitive in its price range.

Victor machines invariably add two and two and get four. But as Victor celebrated its 50th anniversary, the corporation was set up so that it all added up to more than that. Two plus two equaled five, at least. The word was synergism. For instance, Victor had the adding machines and calculators to do the basic work on raw data. And the cash registers sophisticated enough to keep track of sales by clerk, by department, by type of goods and to turn that information over to a computer system for management and inventory control use. The company also had computer units that could collect and process that information. The Victor business schools could train people to operate the various pieces of equipment while the Victor temporary help offices might supply people for extra duty. In addition, its business forms plants were producing forms for every business application including the vast needs of the computers. And there was the Electrowriter, matched

Raymond F. Koch (left),
secretary, and Vincent G. McDonagh,
treasurer, view new Victor Series
1500 electronic printing calculator.

to growing communications needs; and with its companion, Victor Electrowriter Remote Blackboard (VERB), it serves the increasing demands of the educational field.

Victor was also making strides in its second great area of activity: recreational products and toys. In the anniversary year, this division of the company succeeded in generating the larger part of the sales gain and its total sales were expected to reach about $50 million, more than the entire Victor annual volume in 1960.

Victor could be measured by a number of outside and objective yardsticks. For instance, there was the fact that the company was included in *Fortune* magazine's list of the nation's 500 largest U.S. industrial corporations for the year 1967. It was ranked 485th on sales of $139,280,000. Significantly, it was ranked 108th in terms of income as a percent of sales and 69th in terms of income as a percent of invested capital. Victor's rate of growth for the years 1957 through 1967 put it in 87th place among the 500.

But, as A.C. said at the annual meeting of stockholders in 1968, he was not so much interested in where the company has been as in where it is going. Or, as A.C. put it: "On March 8 of this year, Victor entered its second half-century. Since I have been associated with the company for 47 of its 50 years, I can personally testify that we passed this historic milestone with considerably more confidence than we had in 1921—when my father turned me loose on a program of trying to make Victor Adding Machine Co. a success.

"I feel a little like a mountain climber must feel three-fourths of the way to the top. The only difference is that I don't think Victor is three-fourths of the way to the top—for there is no real ceiling on how far we can go in the years ahead."

During Victor's anniversary year, it developed a 10-year program of growth and progress for the company. What concerned the directors and officers as much as anything was the manage-

ment team that would provide the spirit and leadership to carry
the company forward. Commenting on this, A.C. says: "The
main thing is to build a team for 10 years from now. Ball teams
fall apart; they have a series of good years, they go so far and something happens. We're no different, it can happen to us. Except
that we can do more about it. We're in good shape and we intend
to be in better shape."

Always, and increasingly in recent years, the company has carried out the program inaugurated by A.C. years ago of building its
management team by giving its men responsibility and authority
on the firing line. The top corporate officers, the divisional operating heads, the supervisors of profit and cost centers, have been
given a challenge and an opportunity to develop.

A.C. has tried to spend at least two days a week at his farm amid
the rolling, wooded hills outside suburban Barrington, Illinois.
Once there, he refuses anything but the most urgent call from his
office. He will check with his efficient secretary and get a rundown
on the callers and the problems. "Tell him I said to handle it himself," is the usual message. This thought has long characterized
A.C.'s standard operating procedure both when he is seated behind his desk at the office and when he is away from it.

One specific example of the effectiveness of Victor's operating
team is illuminating. In the summer of 1967, low-priced foreign
adding machines were flooding into the American market, under-
cutting the popular, small adders and subtractors in the low end of
the Victor line.

Bert Buehler, as president of the Business Machines Group,
and Theo Fox, the sales vice president, surveyed the situation,
balanced unit costs, profit margins, volume and overhead. With
president Bakewell's approval, they decided Victor should reduce
prices. A.C. found out about the decision only when the information was included in one of the standard reports crossing his desk.

He couldn't have been more pleased, especially since this procedure had been followed on many occasions in the past and always proved to be successful. Indeed, while unit profit margins were squeezed, the anticipated sales increase historically could restore or even increase total profit.

"This is not a one-man operation," A.C. says emphatically, and, eyes twinkling, he offers further proof: "Every year when I go to Arizona for my vacation, they turn in one of the best months of the year just to show me what they can do."

At the other end of the spectrum it is interesting to watch A.C. presiding over a meeting of the board of directors when an important policy decision or a major corporate action such as an acquisition is up for discussion. His tendency is to sit back and let others lead the debate. One of those A.C. depends upon is Vernon R. Loucks, a prominent Chicago lawyer, who handled Carl Buehler's estate and who has been with Victor for decades both as counsel and as a member of the board. Loucks has been invaluable over the years, particularly in the years of the great growth through acquisitions, in pointing out the legal and tax advantages or disadvantages in a proposal and, thus, in turning the discussion toward a "yes" or a "no." Among others on the board are Edward M. Cummings, a vice president of the Continental Illinois National Bank and Trust Company of Chicago and Harold P. O'Connell, a retired Continental Illinois senior vice president. O'Connell, on the board since 1957, is especially apt with his lifetime knowledge of the business world in pointing out the negatives and the pitfalls in proposed acquisitions and in the entry into new fields.

A.C. lets the talk flow freely. Perhaps the negative pinpointed by O'Connell remains standing as an overwhelming factor. Perhaps, on the other hand, Bake or Bert, stimulated by the debate, sees a way around the problem or a way that the resources of Victor can speedily convert a disadvantage into an advantage.

Inside the board room, and outside, A.C. has no wish to short-circuit the thinking process nor to kill off ideas and initiative by injecting his own thinking prematurely.

In any event, as Victor reached its 50th birthday and looked to the future, it not only had bricks and mortar, money and products, but it also had competent and well-motivated men on the production line, in a far-flung distribution system and throughout management. Of all the ingredients of Victor's success, perhaps the motivation of the Victor people is the most important.

For most men, Victor as it stood on its 50th anniversary would have been enough. But not for A.C., or for its management in general. The time A.C. spends away from his office desk is specifically devoted to thinking about Victor's future and to reading business information, suggestions from the staff, material on the general economy and on industry trends, and detailed reports on possible merger candidates. It is time dedicated to helping present management in finding ways to expand and improve what Victor already has in the house and to the consideration of acquisitions that might fit in with Victor's structure and markets.

In addition to its people (more than 8,000), Victor did indeed have bricks and mortar and the organization necessary to continue its historic pattern of growth into its second half century of corporate life. With a total of 18 plants in the United States and Canada, Victor in 1967 invested more than $6,000,000 for the future in expanding certain plants and for machinery and equipment. It expected to invest an additional $5,000,000 in 1968. The Business Machines Group, still accounting for the largest percentage of total sales despite the sharp increase turned in by the recreational products division, is selling through 84 company-owned branch offices, 700 factory-trained franchised sales and service representatives, and some 10,000 retail outlets. In addition, Electrowriter communications systems reach their market through

Victor's 1968 Board of Directors at annual
meeting. Albert C. Buehler, chairman,
seated. Standing, left to right: Albert C.
Buehler, Jr., Alvin F. Bakewell, Cass S.
Hough, Vernon R. Loucks, Lloyd Drexler,
Edward M. Cummings, Raymond J. Koch,
Harold P. O'Connell, Carl Buehler III.

a separate sales organization with offices in 28 major cities, temporary office help is available through 77 offices, and there are 69
Comptometer Schools.

Products of the Business Forms Group are marketed through
43 direct sales offices and some 1,500 dealer outlets.

Recreational products and toys are distributed through approximately 50,000 retail outlets, including 7,000 golf pro shops.

Virtually everything in the Victor line of products for business,
recreation and play is also distributed in Canada. The Victor International Group has 175 major sales outlets in 77 nations of the
free world, and the figuring machines and other products and
services for business it sells outside the United States account for
about 10 percent of the company's total sales. As the other nations
of the world have prospered and moved more and more into the
age of office automation, gains have been made in Victor's foreign
sales. Recreational products and toys, too, are finding their way
into more and more global outlets.

In thinking about Victor, 1968, A.C. settled on the phrase "integrated diversification" as most descriptive of the company's
present status and future direction.

Victor is firmly established in its two great and lively areas of
growth. One is business products and services, everything from the
figuring machines to cash registers to business forms to Electrowriter communications and educational systems to temporary help
services and business education. The second growth area is recreational products, golf, the Daisy line, toys, archery and fishing
tackle. The 60,000,000 men, women, boys and girls now participating in the joys of fishing alone show the potential of that recreational products segment of Victor's business.

The two diverse areas of the Victor enterprise are integrated
into a whole through a small, well-knit corporate officer staff and
a strong system of reporting, control and profit responsibility that

still provides maximum flexibility with corporate support.

A.C., the board of directors, and top management agree that Victor should not be turned into an undisciplined conglomerate. Future acquisitions are expected to complement product lines in one or the other of Victor's fields. They would broaden the product lineup, fill in gaps, and enable Victor to present an integrated face in each market place. Certainly, new and improved products will be developed internally and find their niche, too. And the company can see further opportunities for integrating, and thereby strengthening, the existing sales forces, particularly in the young and growing leisure-time sector.

Explaining all this, A.C. is full of ideas and plans: "You might say that we got into the leisure-time field accidentally because Comptometer already had the golf business when we acquired it. Everything we've done since fits in. Our golf people were selling mainly through golf professionals, but another substantial part of the golf business moves through sports and department stores. That's just where Daisy is strong, so the Daisy marketing organization can help out our golf people.

"When we took on Daisy, its Heddon division was selling only medium and high-priced fresh water fishing tackle. We encouraged them to broaden the line to include salt water tackle and also a line of lower-priced tackle. Then, there's Bear with its high-priced archery sets and Ertl with its toys selling mainly through farm equipment dealers, but with a big area for growth through department stores. You can see right away how we can fit some of these things together. For instance, the Bear salesman was calling on the very top stores with his high-priced bows. We can give him the top line of Heddon fishing tackle and Daisy products to sell to the same stores.

"And we are taking some of the Daisy men who, perhaps, didn't do too much in the toy department with Daisy's line of toy pistols and holsters and we are making full-time toy salesmen out of them by giving them the Ertl models to sell.

"It's working out that way in a number of instances. And you've also got things like the fact that Daisy buys aluminum castings outside and now we have Ertl, an expert in aluminum castings.

"We don't want to become a full-line company in this area. That is, we have no interest in making everything from sports shirts to football shoulder pads to cruisers. But we are interested in companies that make the standard or stable products, both in sports and toys, that we can sell nationally with the sales organizations we have now. This holds true for business machines and services, too.

"In this business, in any business, if you're going to be successful, you've got to have something up your sleeve. You've got to give your salesmen something new to sell if you want to keep their enthusiasm up to par and you've got to offer the public new and better products.

"I said early in this business that if all we could do was to make an adding machine that was no different from the other adding machines on the market, we had no right to be in the business. We had to find a different product, either a different kind or one that would do the same things for less money or one that had more features. One reason the Business Machines Group moved into the position it did is that we kept on bringing out something new and different. And better. I hate to go out and try to sell the same thing the other guy has at the same price. And we won't do it.

"In the Business Machines Group, we've got two new electromechanical calculators coming along. They have new and advanced features to bolster our traditional product line. They should form the base for a whole new family of products just as our computer line and electronic calculators may father a new line of electronic products. We are also putting more time, money and people into the work of the Victor Electronics and Research Center than ever before. In addition, the research center benefits greatly from working with the people in Sweden at Hugin Kassa-register and with the researchers at Nixdorf.

"We have momentum throughout the Business Machines Group. For instance, with improved models on the market we had a 25 percent increase in sales of Digit-Matic units in 1967 and this trend carried over into 1968. We're really just beginning in the cash register field, but we have new models on the market and we're moving into such things as data processing systems based on the cash register.

"All this, what we have and what we can see ahead, adds up. Going back to the beginning, I've been a believer in the idea that you make money in the long run by building up volume on good products.

"I wouldn't want to guess where we will be two years, five years or any other time down the road. But in a free competitive economy, a company's only long-term advantage lies in its human resources. Other advantages that arise from technology, new markets or lower costs are relatively short-lived. So basically it is the dedication, initiative and motivation of people that Victor has relied on the past 50 years and which we will continue to depend on to bring success in the years that lie ahead. This has always been our creed and I hope that we never change."

PUBLISHED BY

Victor Comptometer Corporation

PRINTED AND BOUND BY

R. R. Donnelley & Sons Company
The Lakeside Press

Designed by Robert Gatechair